Starting Rite

For Rob, Lucy and Michael

Starting Ri✝e

First steps in spiritual nurture:
a five-session course for
new parents and babies

Jennifer Paddison

CHURCH HOUSE
PUBLISHING

Church House Publishing
Church House
Great Smith Street
London SW1P 3AZ

Emails: copyright@churchofengland.org.uk

Images on pages 15, 35, 68 and 155 © Elizabeth Michael Photography
http://elizabethmichael.com

ISBN 978 0 7151 4726 9

Typeset by Regent Typesetting
Printed and bound by
CPI Group (UK) Ltd, Croydon

Contents

Acknowledgements

To Bobby Kneen Swinhoe and Sarah May Corry White, the first-ever babies to take a Starting Rite course, and to their lovely mums, Sarah and Alison. Indeed to all the babies and mums, dads, nans who have joined in with Starting Rite over the last three and a half years. To all the people who run the West Newcastle Sure Start children's centres, especially Heather Armstrong; the super groups they ran sparked off our thinking.

Before running the first course, I went to introduce the concept to our Diocesan Mission Enabler. Just before our meeting I prayed that if this was what God wanted, the person I was about to meet would be excited by it. That person was the Revd Barry Hill. Afterwards he sent me an email saying the idea left him 'on a real buzz all day!' Thank you, Barry, for always being encouraging and supportive and for your help in writing Chapter 1.

To the Revd Dr Sandra Millar, Head of Projects for the Church of England. Sandra has been amazing. She came to visit a Starting Rite group two years ago and has been the driving force for getting the course from that point to this. The amount of time and effort she has put in (and I'm sure I don't know the half of it) has been incredible. Also thanks to Lucy Moore, for her advice – including the suggestion to contact Sandra in the first place.

To +Paul Butler, for finding time to meet up and discuss Starting Rite and for his invaluable advice about the handouts. Also, for his encouragement.

To Adam Kent from Sage, Gateshead; and Hannah Farrow from Kevin Mayhew, for giving permission for songs to be reproduced; and to Rachel Shepherd from Lion Hudson, and Marion Zebedee-Topham from Scripture Union, for permission to use images of their children's Bibles. Also to Liz Domokos from Elizabeth Michael photography for her stunning pictures and her permission to use them on the handouts.

To our local health visitors, Angie Bell and Jan Moss, for their advice to mums and leaders.

To Wendy Parmenter and her team at St Mary's Nanpantan for their feedback on running a Starting Rite course in another context.

To three fantastic editors: Tracey Messenger, who helped shape this into a proper book; Elizabeth Hinks for her astonishing eye for detail; and huge thanks to Rebecca Goldsmith who has had to answer my really stupid questions again and again and again.

To Pat Wood, Karen Turner and Alison White, who have been part of Starting Rite from the beginning. They have wiped changing mats, swept up sand, checked water temperatures, cuddled babies, prayed, laughed and made cups of tea with me all through these courses. Thank you.

To Alison White (yet again) for her contribution to the final chapter of this book and for her friendship.

Finally to my husband Rob, who has been constantly positive and forward-looking about Starting Rite. Thank you for being so unselfishly generous about it, especially during difficult times, and always seeing its potential.

Foreword

Starting Rite is a fresh, innovative, courageous, exciting and thoroughly theologically grounded way of helping parents and carers who might be thinking about having a child baptized, or are simply interested in Christian spirituality as part of their child's wellbeing. No longer does a babysitter need to be found while the session is taking place; the baby is at the heart of the programme and, awake or asleep, takes a full part in it with their carer. Goodbye to baptism preparation that, at its worst, involves embarrassing interrogations between strangers or one-way lectures about the baptism service. Welcome to a gentle, empowering, hospitable and, more than anything, *relational* approach that draws not only on knowledge of what baptism is all about, but on current thinking in child psychology and parenting. It's the sort of course that makes me wonder why have I never come across anything like this before?

I was introduced to Jenny several years ago by members of Leicester Diocese's Mission Team who were enthusiastic about her approach to parents, babies and spirituality. I was deeply impressed by her original yet entirely logical ideas and her hands-on experience. Her approach resonates with so much of what churches are finding effective for creating lasting friendships and a firm base for family discipleship within Messy Churches, though it certainly has a far wider reach than this and will, I know, be a rewarding way ahead for many types of congregations. When Revd Dr Sandra Millar started her role as Head of Projects and Development for the Church of England, I knew Jenny was a key thinker who Sandra would appreciate meeting, and I am thrilled that this book that has come out of their conversation means that Jenny's ideas are available more widely.

What we see in the UK today is not a line of parents in secure relationships waiting anxiously to find out from the expert vicar how to instil knowledge of the Christian faith into their children. It's not a trickle of the meek and respectful creeping into church, agog to hear the words of wisdom that drop like precious gems from the minister's lips. It's not a group of people who humbly plead to be enlightened, chastised for their lack of churchgoing and, duly repentant, gratefully taking their place in a suitably lowly corner of the church building until one day in the dim and distant future they may be called to Higher Things, such as being allowed to take the collection. I exaggerate, but still …

The carers we see are the ones Jenny knows as she leads these courses. They may be busy and burdened with the pressures of trying to be brilliant career people as well as brilliant parents. They may have student loans and hefty mortgages to pay off. They may have little time together as a family. They may be conscious of the mountainous quantities of research and advice around bringing up babies that is bewilderingly contradictory. They may live far away from extended family – or worry about asking for too much childcare from grandparents who live nearby. They may be managing alone or without the opportunity to reflect wholesome relationships to their children. And they care desperately about the well-being of their baby. They are of a generation that has instant access to data from around the world at the tap of a Smartphone: they have scant regard for traditional authority that says something is true 'because I say so'. They have less and less family tradition of bringing children to baptism. In a world that reports stories of religious extremism, they are protective. These carers are perhaps not so much interested in 'what to believe' as doing all they can to give their babies the best possible start in life. They are used to learning through experience, talking and online chatting. (And if personal recollection of those days serves, they are probably suffering from severe sleep deprivation, haven't yet realized that there is a long sinister stain on their shoulder just out of eye view, and that while all the other mums have dutifully brought a nice, soft, clean, fresh towel, theirs was last used to dry the dog after a muddy walk and thoughtlessly thrust back in the airing cupboard because a tantrumming toddler was heading for the bleach. Aaargh, the memories.)

Starting Rite is described humorously, humbly and, more than anything, realistically, with full attention paid to the practical details and enough examples to convince the most sceptical reader that this has been tried and tested and is worth the investment. Just as a Messy Church requires thorough planning and meticulous preparation that has a huge pay-off, this course similarly requires significant investment in time and equipment but is well worth it for the impact it obviously makes on the participants. The thorough exploration of the symbols of baptism done in a relational, participative, narrative way is a far cry from formal catechesis but is obviously proving to be effective. It meets those carers where they are and does what the Church does best: creates a safe space to come close to God together across the generations, strengthening family ties, affirming and gently developing a sense of Christian spirituality – as Jesus did when he insisted the children should come to him in Mark 10.14 – and allowing the child herself to demonstrate what discipleship is about – again as Jesus showed in Mark 9.36. Learning with and from children as well as with and from our peers is something we can be very excited about as a Church. It is an attitude we need to develop more of as we encourage families to be households of faith at home as well as gathered in church. What better place to begin than right at the start?

Lucy Moore
Messy Church Founder
Winchester 2015

Introduction

Imagine yourself sitting cross-legged next to three mums with babies on laps in a blackout tent in semi-darkness. Around the tent are several electric tealights giving pockets of flickering yellow glow. The babies reach for the tealights, enfold them in their pudgy hands and shove them straight onto their teething gums. While the tealight-gnawing is going on, you and the parents talk about choices their children can make in life. What would be the best choice? What would be the worst? In answer to the latter, one mum says 'if W [her baby] decided not to speak to me for some reason'. She talks about relatives who stopped talking to each other, the pain and hurt involved and what that would feel like as a parent. She has (unwittingly perhaps) just touched on one aspect of God's relationship with his people.

This is a snapshot of Starting Rite.

What is Starting Rite?

Starting Rite is a five-session Christian nurture course aimed at carers with babies under the age of one. It borrows from the approach of the many 'baby-focused' courses available for new parents (for example, baby massage, baby singing), but has a more explicit focus on the spiritual nurture of very young children. It provides an environment in which carers can spend one-on-one time with their babies and gives them opportunities to think about and ask questions about their child's spiritual life and development. At different stages in the course, we present and explore some of the symbols and terminology of baptism. As such, it may be used as a pre-baptism nurture course.

Where does Starting Rite come from?

Starting Rite was conceived by an Anglican clergy couple (please excuse the pun!) and started in a middle-of-the-road group of Anglican churches in north Leicestershire. This is not to say that Starting Rite can't work in any other denomination, but simply that Starting Rite and the language, assumptions and theology of this book are grounded predominantly within an Anglican context.

Who is it for?

Starting Rite can be run by any church wishing to develop their ministry to families with young children; it can be used for baptism families; but it works with anyone looking for guidance on children's spiritual nurture. There's much more about thinking through whether it is right for your context in Chapter 1: Thinking about the possibility.

The course itself is aimed at babies and their principal carers. By babies, I mean infants from about three weeks old until they reach their first birthday or until they are so mobile they won't sit or lie still on a changing mat for very long. 'Principal carers' refers to the child's mother or father (adopted or birth) or a grandparent or a foster parent. Whenever the word 'carer' is used in this book, it is meant in this sense.

What does a typical Starting Rite session look like?

The session usually lasts an hour and a half. It is very informal and relaxed with lots of interaction between all the participants, with a particular emphasis on the babies and their rhythm.

Usually we have about eight carers and eight babies sitting on the floor with a leader. During the session, at different points, we sing between 10 and 12 songs suitable for babies, for example 'Can you play at peek-a-boo?' and 'Clap your hands'. The songs generally tie in with the theme of that session.

Near the beginning of the session we read a board book (a book whose pages are made of cardboard) together, in harmony.

In between the songs, we do one or two activities that stimulate the visual and tactile senses. The leader comments briefly on the activity and its connection to Christianity.

At some point during the session, the leader asks one or two questions which involve a short discussion and generally leads to responses being written on post-its to go into baby record books.

At another point during the session, there is some 'free time' for carers to talk among themselves over refreshments. There's a blessing at the end.

The shape of this book

Part 1 Preparing to run Starting Rite

This includes a few theological and logistical questions for you to consider before launching a Starting Rite course, including whether it is right for your context. It also covers all the practicalities of setting up and running a course, including recruiting the right team and thinking through your venue and equipment. We move on to look at how you can advertise and attract families to the group and finally how to resource your Starting Rite programme appropriately.

Part 2 The Starting Rite sessions

The five Starting Rite sessions and their Christian themes are as follows:

1. Peek-a-Boo! – the mystery of God
2. How Much Love? – God's unconditional love
3. Splash! – baptism symbolism
4. Bubble-Talk – prayer
5. Storytime – the Bible

At the beginning of each section on the sessions themselves, I explain the theological background and reasoning behind each game or activity.

The theological basis is followed by the nitty-gritty detail of what actually happens and the equipment required.

Part 3 Next steps

Finally, we consider some other optional ideas for the course; how to take the course further to prepare for baptism and how a church can maintain contact with Starting Rite participants and their families.

How Starting Rite developed

When my oldest child, Lucy, was born, I started attending children's centres in west Newcastle, where we then lived. We followed courses such as Baby Massage, Baby Singing, Baby Yoga, Baby Weaning, Baby Swimming, Baby Health and Social, and Baby Music. Eighteen months later and with another baby on the way, I took a theological course on creativity and spirituality in worship and evangelism. The course challenged us to think creatively about mission and discipleship. My husband observed one day around this time, that there seemed to be 'baby everything under the sun', but nothing particularly spiritual, nothing about faith.

Do babies have a spiritual side? If we baptize them, they must, right? So my husband said why not invent a baby spiritual nurture course? And then he left me to sort it all out.

In order to develop the course, however, I needed to explore a few questions.

Why do parents/carers do these courses?

In order to answer this question, I did some research about children's centres and talked to my own local one.[1]

As mentioned above, Starting Rite arose from my own experience of Sure Start children's centres. Sure Start was an initiative of the last Labour government: the purpose being to 'deliver the best start in life for every child by bringing together early education, childcare, health and family support'.[2] Ofsted inspections reported that the centres fulfilled their role extremely

---

1 The research was undertaken in the summer of 2010; the current situation may be different.

2 http://www.dcsf.gov.uk/everychildmatters/earlyyears/surestart/

well, providing support for families and facilitating learning and health-care both for children and parents.[3]

There were several reasons for their success:

- Depending on employers, mums can take up to a year's maternity leave. This ensures they have time to spend with their baby, and they may well be looking for activities to do with their child.
- In areas of high deprivation, accessibility was key. In urban areas, there would have been at least one within pram-pushable distance of most children.[4]
- The centres promote peer support; gathering adults in similar situations together and facilitating conversation.
- Most significantly, they meet people's needs by offering good-quality activities and by listening to their clients.
- Health visitors inform new parents about what's on at the local centre and encourage them to attend.

What goes on in children's centres?

Some children's centres run a variety of courses and I attended some of these groups with both my babies. Some are rolling programmes, run weekly; some, for example, Baby Massage, Baby Yoga and Baby Weaning, are short, weekly courses that run over 3–6 weeks. The numbers of parents who attended these with their children at my local children's centre speak for themselves: Baby Health and Social (aimed at babies between 0 and 1) attracted an average of 18 mums every week over 50 weeks; Baby Massage: 12 over 5 weeks; Baby Yoga: 10 over 5 weeks.[5] There were waiting lists to attend the latter two courses. These courses were totally baby-centred, concentrating on sensori-motor thought and experience: movement, music,

---

3 www.surestart.gov.uk *A Sure Start Children's Centre for Every Community; Phase 2 Planning Guidance (2006–2008)*, 4 and 12 and www.ofsted.gov.uk/Ofsted-home/Publications-and-research/Browse-all-by/Documents-by-type/Thematic-reports/ *The impact of integrated services on children and their families in Sure Start Children's Centres* (Ofsted Publications, July 2009), 9 and 10.

4 *A Sure Start Children's Centre for Every Community*, 6. Again the current situation may be different.

5 Statistics gathered from Sure Start Fenham Children's Centre at Sacred Heart and Stocksfield Avenue School, academic year, 2009–10.

light and touch. The leaders guided and accompanied the mothers and their babies through the exercises or activities; the idea was that the parent would continue the activities with their child at home.

I surveyed the mums in the Baby Health and Social group at my local children's centre and asked them why they came to the group. The two main reasons given were 'to do something different and interesting with their baby' and 'to get out of the house'. These baby-centred courses are clearly popular and meet their objectives. However, as my husband noted, a large gap was evident in terms of faith development.

Why is 'play' so important in terms of a baby's development?

If you don't have much contact with babies, spend a morning with one and their carer. Nothing beats the hands-on experience of cuddles and dealing with poo and regurgitated milk. It will give you an insight into the non-verbal, largely experiential and 'play-full' world of babies. Peter Privett, in *Through the Eyes of a Child*, notes how paradoxical it is to *write* or *talk* about play, as 'play for children operates in the non-logical, non-verbal realms of language. The real difficulty is in the translation process … Adults prefer to operate in the logical world, the world of words and ideas. Original visions can vanish, in the telling, in the adult-eration.'[6]

It's a bit like when someone is relating a moment or incident that evoked strong emotion (hilarity, terror or awe), but the narration of the event spectacularly fails to raise similar feelings in the audience and the narrator trails off by saying 'you had to be there'. With babies, you really have to be there. Once you see the world through the eyes of a baby, you will see the rationale behind Starting Rite.

If you would like to read more about the development of babies as part of your thinking about running a Starting Rite course, please see Further Reading and Bibliography on p. 174.

When I was pregnant, all expectant mothers were given the NHS publication *Birth to Five*; nowadays there are webpages with videos: www.nhs. uk/Conditions/pregnancy-and-baby/pages/play-ideas-and-reading.aspx. Both explain the vital importance of play for babies:

---

6 Anne Richards and Peter Privett (eds), 2009, *Through the Eyes of a Child*, London: Church House Publishing, p. 101.

Play is important to children as it is spontaneous, and in their play children use the experiences they have and extend them to build up ideas, concepts and lifelong skills that they can carry with them in later life. While playing, babies and children can try things out, solve problems, take risks and use trial and error to find things out and be creative.

Babies and children have to experience play physically and emotionally. In other words, it is not enough to provide stuff to play with. The most important element for young babies is the parent or primary caregiver. It is that person who forms a close emotional bond with the baby. A child with this secure attachment feels able to rely on their parents or caregivers for safety and comfort, develops knowledge about communication and language, and uses these important attachment relationships as bases from which to explore and learn about the world.[7]

Advice on the web and in the book is given to parents about what to do with their child. Here are a few examples:

- 'Even babies and small children like other children's company … Ask your health visitor if there is a new parents' group meeting in your area. Getting together with other parents can be good for you too.'
- 'Make sure there are times when you focus completely on your child.'
- 'Get together lots of different things for your child to look at, think about and do.'
- 'As your baby grows, have fun singing nursery rhymes and songs, especially those with actions like "Pat-a-cake" and "Row, row, row your boat".'
- 'Play games where you have to take turns, like peek-a-boo and round and round the garden.'
- 'Let your baby lie down and kick their legs.'
- 'Toys that your child can pick up and move around will help improve their coordination and develop the muscles in their arms and hands.'
- 'You can start looking at books with your baby from an early age … Even quite small babies like looking at picture books … Looking at books with your child, even if it's just for 10 minutes a day, will help them build important skills and encourage their interest in reading.'[8]

---

7 NHS, *Birth to Five*, produced by COI for the Department of Health. To view, visit: http://webarchive.nationalarchives.gov.uk/+/www.dh.gov.uk/en/Publicationsandstatistics/ Publications/publicationspolicyandguidance/DH_107303, click on chapter 5, Learning and Playing, pp. 74ff.

8 NHS, *Birth to Five*, pp. 68, 74ff.

I was reading my own copy of the NHS publication for information about how to help my little ones, but I was also reading books about children's spirituality at the same time. In particular, the work of Rebecca Nye, a psychologist who is an expert on children's spirituality. Among other points, she notes that spirituality emphasizes process not product:

> Production suggests that the end result is all important, and that this kind of work can be finished ... But spiritual life is an on-going piece of work, not something to be completed or get prizes for ... Process honours the present moment too, and learning to be fully present. Similarly, childhood deserves to be treated as a process rather than a production line for delivering adults, or Christians.[9]

Generally speaking, we can observe that babyhood is all about process. Babies are valued for who and how they are right at that moment, not for what they can achieve in the future, nor for doing things 'properly'; and most of all baby and carer live in the present. There are many other aspects of spirituality that parents (of any faith or none) delight in when seeing them in their children. Rebecca Nye, quoting the Christian educator Sofia Cavalletti, identifies '*deep joy* and a sense of *pure wonder* as core strengths in children's spirituality capacities'.[10] Parents (for themselves and their children) are also very likely to care profoundly about the ability to make sense of the world and life[11] and 'to reflect on areas which are beyond those of individual/ego interest'.[12] These are both definitions of spirituality.

So it seemed to me that in many ways it made complete sense for the Church to encourage and foster spirituality in babies in a similar way to those courses and groups run in children's centres.

---

9 Rebecca Nye, *Children's Spirituality*, London: Church House Publishing, 2009, pp. 47–8.

10 Nye, *Children's Spirituality*, pp. 76–7.

11 Nye, *Children's Spirituality*, quoting Clive Erricker, p. 3.

12 Nye, *Children's Spirituality*, quoting Margaret Donaldson, p. 3.

What are the issues that church leaders struggle with around the whole area of baptism?

Much has been written and lamented about the challenges facing the Church concerning the ministry of baptism and the loss of children and young people from its congregations. Here are a few concerns:

• Some families appear to 'treat baptism as some kind of 'wash and go';[13] after the baptism, they are never seen again at church.
• Concern is often expressed that the sacrament of baptism is being devalued because of lack of engagement by the participants.[14]
• While some see baptism and outreach to new parents as 'an amazing missionary opportunity',[15] there is also a perception that the baptism service itself is wordy, heavily liturgical and not particularly mission-oriented.
• Even some Christian parents are unsure how to nurture faith in their children.[16]

You may be able to think of many more.

Think for a moment about your own baptism preparation and consider the following questions. When you talk to families about baptism:

• Do you see this as a mission and nurture opportunity?
• How much do you focus on the child?
• To what extent do you feel the family's understanding or appreciation of the sacrament has increased?
• How much difference does it make in their Christian journey?
• To what extent do you feel a relationship has been established between them and the church?
• Do you ever receive feedback or appreciation of your baptism preparation?

---

13 Paul Bayes, Tim Sledge et al., *Mission-Shaped Parish*, London: Church House Publishing, 2006, p. 53.

14 Stephen Kuhrt, *Church Growth Through the Full Welcome of Children*, Cambridge: Grove Books, 2009, p. 9.

15 Bayes and Sledge, *Mission-Shaped Parish*, p. 55.

16 John Drane, *The McDonaldization of the Church*, London: Darton, Longman and Todd, 2000, p. 59.

I used to feel fairly frustrated about how inadequate my baptism preparation was and how difficult it was to convey some of the concepts involved. This dissatisfaction fed into the development of Starting Rite.

How can 'play' be used to nurture children's faith and spirituality? And could the symbols of baptism – oil, water, light – be used as part of children's play?

The last two questions have been answered together, because by this point Starting Rite had really started to take shape and theoretical and practical ideas were already being woven together.

As already explored, Starting Rite borrows from the excellent early years' group activities that the Sure Start children's centres and other courses on offer for new parents provide. These all provide opportunities for parents to follow the advice as set out in the NHS book and facilitate 'learning and health-care both for children and parents'. It is important to note that the Sure Start children's centres' emphasis is on intellectual and physical development. The Starting Rite course offers the same style of group activity but focuses on the *spiritual*. It is a baby-centred approach to preparing families for baptism, but more importantly for the Christian journey beyond.

When we consider our sacraments, the Church has much to be proud of in the face of the recent re-emphasis on the experiential. For two millennia, the Church has used the senses to convey the truths of our faith through light, water, oil, food and drink. Of course our faith demands our intellect: the reading and interpretation of Scripture, theological reflection and reasoning and what the practical and ethical outworkings of this thinking might look like.

However, the word is not the only way in which God comes to us; God also meets us in our everyday, lived experiences. Jesus used ordinary things to show what God was like, by telling stories and parables involving agri-cultural and farming references, household objects, precious stones and money, food and parties. He even compared our relationship with him to that of children and their games (Luke 7.31–32). Theological concepts lend themselves to experiential analogy.

All the play or activities in Starting Rite have a theological rationale behind them. They work as a sort of 'play-metaphor' for a particular aspect of our faith or lived experience of being a Christian. What I mean by this is the game or play we engage in represents either what it is like being a Christian or what God is like. So, for example, recalling the scene right at the start of this introduction, in the third session, Splash!, we sit in the blackout tent with the tealights and discuss good and bad choices in life. From birth, babies naturally turn towards light;[17] the darkness of the tent and the tealights are used to illustrate the liturgy in the baptism service:

'In baptism, God calls us out of darkness into his marvellous light.'
'I turn to Christ.'
'You have received the light of Christ; walk in this light all the days of your life.'

The questions about choices explore the outworkings of that 'turning away from darkness and towards light'.

The chewing over of all the answers led to a rough shape of the first Starting Rite course. At this point it was called SpiriBabes and was trialled with a couple of church mums and babies. We talked about how they felt the course would be received by others and they were (bless them) encouraging. So I started running it for baptism and any other interested families. It continued to be shaped and developed, and no doubt will need further adjustments. Feedback from participants is received after every course and (so far at least!) has been positive.

The main aims of Starting Rite

Starting Rite covers a variety of objectives, but its two main aims are:

1. To give parents or carers an opportunity to focus on their baby.
2. To equip them for the nurture of their child's Christian faith.

Why are these important?

---

17 Kaz Cooke, *The Rough Guide to Babies and Toddlers*, London: Penguin, 2009, p. 199.

Giving carers the opportunity to focus on their baby

Carers on maternity leave enjoy spending quality, constructive time with their babies. If it's their first child, they are looking for ideas and advice for the development of their little one and the opportunity to meet other parents/carers. If it's their second or third, they feel a need to give exclusive time and attention to their youngest. Our faith, in Scripture and Church tradition, points to the importance of parental responsibility, of community involvement with the raising of children, of developing children's education, health and faith. Starting Rite joins in that long tradition within churches of fostering and encouraging child–parent relationships.

Equipping parents/carers for the nurture of their child's Christian faith

Give ear, O my people, to my teaching;
incline your ears to the words of my mouth.
I will open my mouth in a parable;
I will utter dark sayings from of old,
things that we have heard and known,
that our ancestors have told us.
We will not hide them from their children;
we will tell to the coming generation
the glorious deeds of the Lord, and his might,
and the wonders that he has done. (Psalm 78.1–4)

We do not live in an age where telling our children about 'the glorious deeds of the Lord' happens over the cornflakes; the telling of our Christian stories has declined dramatically over many generations. And yet, three-year-olds still ask questions such as, 'Why do we have to die?' What meaningful answer can a parent give if they don't have a faith? Even if they do have a faith, are they able to respond appropriately? Many carers have asked me to reply to questions that their pre-school children have asked, such as 'How did God make me, when actually Mummy and Daddy did?'; 'How was God made?'/ 'Did God make himself?'; 'Where is God?'; 'Why can't we see God?' The parents themselves have struggled to know how to respond. Some could articulate answers but not in a way a child would understand; some were unsure that their answers were 'right' and some did not feel able to answer the questions at all.

Starting Rite begins the process of equipping parents with tools to respond to their children's spiritual needs.

Hopefully this introduction will have given you an idea of:

- How Starting Rite ties in with child development (see pp. 6–11).
- How Starting Rite meets the needs of babies and caregivers (see pp. 12–13).
- How the play-metaphors potentially offer parents a 'way in' to Christian thought, belief or practice (this is looked at in more detail in the session structures themselves).

The rest of this book aims to explain how Starting Rite can work for you.

Part 1

Preparing to run Starting Rite

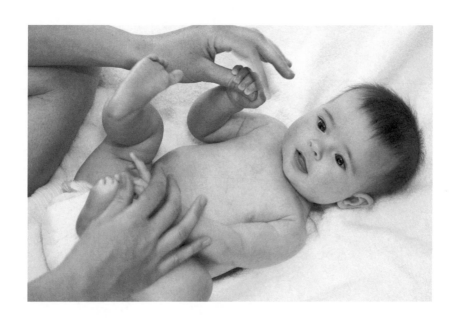

1

Thinking about the possibility

You're probably wondering if Starting Rite would suit your context and actually work in your church.

This chapter considers: what Starting Rite values and how this might fit with your values as a church; what kind of church and community you are in and how Starting Rite might work practically in your situation.

What are the values of Starting Rite?

Starting Rite values babies and family

As already stated, one of two main aims of Starting Rite is to give parents or carers an opportunity to focus on their baby.

The key difference between Starting Rite and most other forms of baptism preparation is that it is baby-focused. Much of the time in Starting Rite sessions should allow mums or principal carers to dedicate their full attention to their child.

But Starting Rite is part of the church's wider ministry; it provides a link between the family and the church community, so the church as a whole also has a role to play in valuing babies and their families.

Questions for you to consider:

How does your church currently welcome babies and their families at baptism services?

How does your church currently welcome and involve babies and their families at other services?

How would your congregation welcome a potential increase in the number of babies (and their crying) attending your church? Be honest.

Would your church community be prepared to engage personally with the Starting Rite participants by chatting with and cooing over them while serving a lunch?

Starting Rite values baptism[18]

Starting Rite works on the premise that infant baptism, in the delightfully whimsical language of 1662, is 'most agreeable'.[19] At least two of the sessions concentrate on aspects of the baptism service with a view to explaining the sacrament more meaningfully to the participants. But let's also note the Pastoral Introduction to the service of Holy Baptism in *Common Worship*:

> Baptism marks *the beginning* of a journey with God which continues for the rest of our lives, the *first* step in response to God's love.[20]

The second main aim of Starting Rite, therefore, is to equip parents for the nurture of their child's Christian faith.

The course can be used as part of your preparation for the christening service, but the Starting Rite emphasis is on encouraging and helping families

---

18 As this book deals almost exclusively with babies, I use the terms *baptism* and *christening* interchangeably.

19 Book of Common Prayer, Articles of Religion, XXVII. Of baptism: 'The Baptism of young children is in any wise to be retained in the Church, as most agreeable with the institution of Christ.'

20 *Common Worship: Services and Prayers for the Church of England*, London: Church House Publishing, 2000, p. 345 (my italics).

with the *long-term* exploration of their faith. In this respect it upholds the words from the Prayer of Commission in the *Common Worship* baptism service:

Together with all God's people
you must explore the way of Jesus
and grow in friendship with God.[21]

Saying all of this, our experience of running Starting Rite is that the course does generate more baptisms for babies and toddlers. We have found that people who attended without thinking about christening have subsequently decided to take the plunge (as it were) and that participants who come from outside our parish sometimes want to have their children christened in our church rather than their own because, as they themselves have said, 'We know you.' We encourage them to talk this through with their particular parish priest before agreeing to hold the christening in our church.

Questions for you to consider:

What does your church think about infant baptism?

How does your church currently prepare families for christenings?

How would Starting Rite fit in with that baptism preparation?

What are your neighbouring parishes' policies on infant baptism? (This is important because neighbouring vicars might prefer families from their parish to have the children baptized in their church and this should be respected.)

Starting Rite values the Bible

The main theological focus of Starting Rite is exploring and reflecting on our relationship with God and it is good to do this with an understanding of the history of that relationship. So Starting Rite takes seriously the biblical

---

21 *Common Worship*, p. 359.

instruction to pass on our knowledge of God from generation to generation.[22]

The Storytime session

Session 5 of the course, Storytime, concentrates on explaining Bible stories
and how we can understand them. It focuses on three stories: the Lost Sheep;
the Wise and Foolish Builders, and the Exodus.

I explain in more depth why these three stories were chosen for this session
in the introduction to the Storytime session. But one word on the choice of
the Exodus story. The Exodus is crucial to our (and, of course, the Jewish)
faith. It has been told to children, and their children, and their children's
children for 4,000 years more or less. I don't know about you, but I find that
deeply thrilling.

Handouts

At the end of every session, handouts are given to carers for them to peruse
at their leisure. All the handouts make reference to the Bible. Some point
out what the Bible says about the topic covered in that session and one of
them suggests parents read a psalm. The Storytime handout, with its specific
emphasis on Scripture, encourages parents to read Bible stories to their
children, gives guidelines on how to choose children's Bibles and gives a list
of recommended children's Bibles.

Questions for you to consider:

What place does your church give to Scripture?

Do you have Bible study groups in your church?

How does your church hand on Bible stories to the children in your
congregation and parish?

---

22 See Deuteronomy 4 and 11 particularly, but also Psalm 78 quoted in the Introduction.

Starting Rite values the Church

Starting Rite values Church tradition and church community.

Church tradition

There are many symbols and signs that the Church has used through the centuries to communicate our faith. Some are used almost universally: water for baptism; candles as the light of Christ; bread and wine/juice for communion. Starting Rite picks up on a tradition that has a long history within the Christian and Jewish faiths: the use of oil. The second session in Starting Rite – How Much Love? – looks at unconditional love and we spend most of the session massaging the babies with oil. This is linked to the Church tradition of using oil to anoint newly baptized Christians with the sign of the cross. Anointing with oil goes back a long way; it has its roots in the Old Testament. So while my husband is a typical low, evangelical clergyman when it comes to oils (he wouldn't know his chrisms from his catechumens) even he uses the latter for christenings since we've started running Starting Rite.

Most families will not know the background of this oil: how it is blessed in the Maundy Thursday service and distributed throughout the churches in the diocese; how it is kept in a 'safe'; how it is reserved for baptism candidates. It gives them a sense of something special and precious and that there is a pretty grand story behind it. And not only is their child honoured with this special and precious oil, they have in some way become part of that story – they are part of something bigger. It ties in with the sense that God makes the ordinary extraordinary, that sacraments are everyday visible objects containing something awesome and invisible.

Church community

Below are two contrasting stories about church welcomes:

Story 1

We run a pram/toddler service on a weekly basis. When one of the pregnant mums who had been attending for a while brought her newborn in, the whole group of mums, grandmums, child-minders and carers broke out in spontaneous applause and there was then a fight over who got to hold the baby first (OK, maybe not fisticuffs, but there was a definite show of triumphalism displayed by the winner). What was being demonstrated was the community's innate desire to welcome and include new arrivals. The message was 'you belong to us'.

Story 2

A long time ago, I had a conversation with a young mum who wanted to have her baby christened. This particular church had decided that baptisms could only be held during the main Sunday morning service. The mum was adamant that she wanted the christening outside the service. During the course of the conversation I probed further into her reluctance to join the main service. After a while, I worked out that she was terrified of being with a group of people she didn't know. She wasn't sure how her other children would behave in the service and she was horrified at having to speak aloud in front of a large group of strangers. She felt that she would be judged. Her perception of the Church's message was 'we don't approve of you and you don't belong'.

This is tragic when we consider that part of the baptism service is an emphasis on welcoming the newly baptized into the church community:

People of God, will you welcome these children/candidates and uphold them in their new life in Christ?
All   **With the help of God, we will.**[23]

Starting Rite aims to build relationship with God, through his people, so the course involves as much as possible people from the church community to help, lead, meet and greet. This can work well with broader baptism ministry. One Sunday after a service, one of the baptism visitors from my church introduced me to a family with the words 'Jenny, SpiriBabes' (which was the name we used for the course at the time). The baptism visitor had previously helped with a SpiriBabes/Starting Rite course and was enthusiastic about it. The mum and baby then attended a course and got to know more of the church community.

---

23 *Common Worship*, p. 353.

One of the unforeseen benefits of Starting Rite is that the carers also get to know each other and we have found that they will support each other by attending one another's baby's christenings. Again this builds up the community, making connections and forming relationships.

Questions for you to consider:

How does your church use symbols and signs in the baptism service? Does your minister or priest use a shell, oil, a white christening robe, and so on?

How does your church view these symbols?

How many people are already involved with your baptism ministry?

Do you have baptism visitors? What is their role?

What is your experience of baptism families and their relationship with church?

Starting Rite values experience

Multisensory experience

There is a huge amount of multisensory input in the Starting Rite course. This involves bringing experience to learning about God: Starting Rite allows babies to explore in a very physical way. Both fine and gross motor skills are developed, through the handling of material, balls, sponges and through song actions, swaying, clapping, lifts and so on. The senses are evoked continually, particularly touch, sight and hearing. Babies themselves add taste to that list by chewing, gnashing, sucking and licking pretty much all the objects on offer. One of my favourite memories of leading Starting Rite is that of a baby girl gnawing a large smooth pebble for a good twenty minutes.

Learning through experience or learning through doing

Starting Rite values experience as a way of learning more about God and following him as Christians. Experience is important for Starting Rite because we do this learning by *doing*. For someone to appreciate what happens at the point of baptism, we could tell the person what to expect: water is poured over the baby's head and some words are said.

But how about if instead of *verbalizing* and *thinking about the idea*, you *actually* plunged a baby into a big tub and allowed them to splash themselves, their parents, you and most of your church premises with oceanic quantities of the good ole' H_2O. Thinking (or reflecting) about the 'doing' and what it means often follows afterwards and, in the Starting Rite case, this may take place largely in the carer's brains rather than the baby's (but then again who knows?).

Learning through experience in community; 'situated learning'[24]

These experiences lead participants to learn more about Christianity but not simply as individuals. If our faith teaches us how to be Christians that involves a shaping of our identity and this can and should take place within the church community.

So Starting Rite encourages and practises the things the Christian community does:

- Singing together
- Reading books together
- Practising routines or rituals together.

The course also facilitates sharing of experiences; the telling of and listening to stories from the participants and also from Christians before us. I am still receiving 'stories' from participants who contact me to tell me about an element raised in Starting Rite that has meaning for them at that point in their life. And when they relate *their* experience, *I* am then learning more about our faith and our God in a way that enriches my own Christian journey and hopefully those of others.

---

24 For more information on this, see: http://infed.org/mobi/jean-lave-etienne-wenger-and-communities-of-practice/

> ## Questions for you to consider:
>
> How does your church use experience in its ministry?
>
> To what extent does your worship include multisensory elements – for example, in its use of music, lights, incense?
>
> Does your church offer opportunities to share experiences that show God's work in your life and the lives of others – for example, people giving testimonies?

Starting Rite values mission

A salutary tale

At one of the baby groups I used to attend with my son, I met a mum who told me how she wanted her child christened. One of the reasons she had sought the Church was because in her words 'I think it would be good for *x* to have something to hold onto in life, like a faith.' She spoke to her local church, who asked her to attend some evenings explaining the Christian faith. She told me that as she did not come from a religious background, she had many questions which she kept asking, but the leaders seemed irritated by her 'interruptions' and flatly dismissed her questions with 'you just have to believe this'.

I was utterly dismayed by this response by the church. If the church can't deal with questions about our faith what kind of faith does it proclaim?

This conversation played a role in shaping Starting Rite, as I felt it important to provide an opportunity for these sorts of questions to be raised and taken seriously and respectfully.

The Church of England enjoys a unique position in terms of service and mission to others. We are often thinking how to reach our neighbours, but in the occasional offices people come to us. And what an amazing privilege that is! I am constantly meeting people who are sympathetic to the idea of faith, and open to encouragement to explore it further.

The Church, contemporary culture and Starting Rite

In terms of mission, it may be quite useful to have an idea of contemporary culture and how it differs from Church culture.

Have a look at the diagram below:[25]

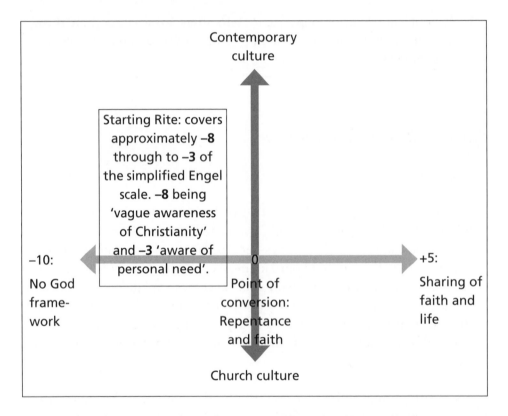

The horizontal axis is the Engel scale (explained below). The vertical axis covers the progression between the worldviews of Church culture and contemporary culture.

---

25 This has been borrowed and adapted from www.theuglyducklingcompany.com and from a simplified version of the Engel scale: www.ywamcampaigns.org/Articles/1000067091/The_Engel_Scale.aspx

Starting Rite and the Engel scale

The Engel scale, if you haven't come across it, basically represents the spectrum between a total absence of belief in God through to a mature Christian faith. So, a person at −10 would be an atheist for example. Starting Rite works with people who are open to encounter Christianity. I always make sure participants are aware that the course is 'religious' (and we employ that word because that is the word they would use). Starting Rite is not 'ambush evangelism'. Rather, it is aimed at those who fall between −8 to −3 on that scale. What I mean by this is that the participants are not adverse to religion, faith or God, that is they are not atheists. It is unlikely that atheists would come on the course, because the subtitle 'you, your baby and God' clearly indicates that it focuses on faith. I have had situations where a participant's partner was atheist and did not attend the final session. Some participants may be agnostic, but some may be very open to exploring Christian beliefs and entering more intentionally into a relationship with God. I am hesitant to make sweeping judgements about all the carers who have undertaken the courses I've led, but I would say that the vast majority fall within those points on the Engel scale. In other words, they may have a vague awareness of Christianity, may have some interest rising to positive experience of Christian love and an awareness of personal need.

On the evaluation forms I used to ask whether participants found the course either 'too religious', 'not religious enough' or 'just right'. Everyone ticked the 'just right' box. I've now removed that question from the form because I feel confident that the course is appropriate for their level of religious engagement.

Starting Rite and contemporary culture

Some aspects of contemporary culture are very much part of the Starting Rite ethos.

Four areas particularly are addressed:

1. Contemporary language and knowledge vs Church language and knowledge

The more I work in ministry, the more I realize that Church language needs to be translated into a vocabulary that a contemporary audience would understand. Lucy Moore in *Messy Church* quotes:

> Oh generous love! that he, who smote
> In Man for man the foe,
> The double agony in man
> For man should undergo.
>
> (Cardinal Newman, 1801–90)

'Brilliant hymn; sung it all my life; I find more in it every time I sing it. But it's not Radio 2, is it?'[26]

Starting Rite aims to translate some of the language of Christianity into the language of child and parenthood. So in one session, we ask about the feelings people have towards their babies. The idea is to use their own vocabulary to explain God's love for us. Not all the terms are appropriate, but expressions such as 'unconditional love', 'very protective', 'I want to be with them more than anything else', 'they're just lovely' come out quite often. The Starting Rite leader may then point out that this is all pretty much how God sees us, only multiplied by a few billion.

Starting Rite assumes that caregivers have little or no knowledge of Christianity or the Bible. (And who am I to judge? I've got a degree in theology and I'm still struggling with that Newman hymn above ...) It's about starting where people are. So if they have never heard of the story of the Lost Sheep, the Wise and Foolish Builders and Moses crossing the Red Sea, they will have by the end of the course. If they don't know how to pray for their children, they'll have some idea by the end of the course. If they don't know what to do when their four-year-old asks 'Where is God?', they will at the very least *not* reply 'Errr, umm, oh look, Waybuloo is on the telly, that's sort of religious' and maybe at best they might sit down and have a chat with them about how together we *can* know God.

---

26 Lucy Moore, *Messy Church*, London: Bible Reading Fellowship, 2006, p. 18.

2. *Exploring vs telling*

Remember the story at the beginning of this section on mission? Church culture traditionally tells people the answers to questions about faith (and in that case also tried to dictate a belief in them). Contemporary culture prefers to have a conversation about it. People encountering our faith for the first time may be at the beginning of a journey, but they are not stupid. You may have carers on your Starting Rite course with little formal education, but that does not deprive them of the ability to think and reflect. Starting Rite does not lecture people about what to believe: it simply invites reflection about God and faith. So questions are asked in all Starting Rite sessions; they make up a small but essential part of the course. The act of listening to the carers' answers respectfully and thoughtfully is crucial to the Starting Rite ethos. To follow up that reflection, handouts are given at the end of the sessions. The handouts elaborate the theme of the session, explaining Christian beliefs and suggesting practical ways of nurturing that aspect of faith as a family.[27] You can always invite feedback from the handouts at the following session, either in the group or in one-to-one conversations.

3. *'Does it work?' vs 'Is is true?'*

In my work as a university chaplain, the president of the Christian Union once told me that members of the CU were struggling with their call to evangelize the campus. When they told their friends with missionary zeal and biblical authority that Jesus died and rose again, their non-Christian friends replied 'So what? I've got a dissertation and two bottles of vodka to finish before tomorrow' (or words to that effect). Church culture can have a tendency to simply assert the truth of its message, as in that example. Contemporary culture asks 'What has that got to do with me?' or even 'What are the benefits for me?' Starting Rite seeks to connect our faith with people's lives. Again this is often an exercise in translation. It is explaining how the good news of our faith makes a difference to a person's life in their situation now.

For mums, dads and carers, it might be any number of things:

- Seeking help about religious questions: 'If your child asks a question about Jesus, and you're not sure how to answer, ask the leader of the church mums and toddler group.'

---

27 The handouts are on the accompanying CD.

- It might be drawing out an aspect of our spiritual make-up, for example, 'Do you feel grateful for the birth of your son/daughter? Is this something you would like to give thanks for? Here is a way of articulating and directing that sense of gratitude … '
- It might be through story, for example: 'Looking at the story of the wise and foolish builders, what are the rocks representing? What makes good foundations for life? What do you feel are important values to encourage in your baby now and as they grow up?'

There is a sense in which the truth of the faith comes through or is demonstrated in the practical application of it.

4. Visual vs textual

Can you remember when newspapers contained columns and columns of words, sentences and paragraphs? Nowadays, due to the Internet and colour printing, newspapers present a more magazine-style appearance with large colour images. The Internet allows news to be shown via a camera roll of pictures or, more frequently nowadays, video clips. News is communicated much more through image now than through text and this reflects the preferences of the current-day consumer.

I have already mentioned in the Introduction how Starting Rite represents a shift away from verbal or textual explanation of baptism and matters of faith towards one that is experienced through play. Starting Rite very much concentrates on visual experience, but its emphasis is also on the tactile, audio and kinesthetic.

A final word on mission

As you see from the Engel scale graph on p. 26, Starting Rite does not take people to the point of conversion (though we'd never stop them!) as an Alpha course might. More thought could be given to appropriate follow-up to a Starting Rite course for both parents and children. Any suggestions are welcome …

Questions for you to consider:

What is your church's attitude to mission?

Does your church see ministry among baptism families as an opportunity for mission?

To what extent would your church feel that there is a tension between contemporary culture and Church culture? And to what extent does that viewpoint inform the way your church undertakes mission?

Does your church run courses that aim to lead people to a point of conversion?

Thinking about your church and community

Your church

In order to run Starting Rite, some thought needs to be given as to how your church will support this initiative. A few starting blocks:

Prayer. Will the church community commit to praying regularly for the courses, its leaders and participants?

Last time we ran a Starting Rite course, one of the intercessors prayed in the main Sunday service for the course and for myself, all the helpers and the families themselves. It was lovely; it made me feel that I was not alone in the task before me and that others cared about the people coming along and their journey towards God.

Leaders. Have you got potential leaders and helpers?

Starting Rite requires one leader and at least one assistant leader (if you want to offer childcare for older siblings, then obviously more helpers are needed). The leader does not have to be in a role of authorized or licensed ministry, but they do need to be able to reflect theologically. This is in order to respond to comments made in answer to questions during the sessions. Don't worry: 'reflecting theologically' sounds much grander than it really is. If a mum said, 'I feel protective about my baby and don't want him hurt', you can just link this to God and how he never wants his creation/people/ children hurt. It's that simple.

The assistant leader's role is vital; not only do they serve hot drinks, help set up and put away, greet mums and hold babies, but they also lead parts of the course (more of that in Session 3, Splash!, pp. 116–27) and contribute to discussions about parenthood and faith.

There is a reasonable amount of lifting, carrying, assembling and cleaning involved in Starting Rite; if your leaders are not physically able to perform such tasks, you will need to find some others willing to help out.

My experience in finding helpers has been very positive. There are a number of selling points when it comes to advertising for volunteers: 1) It's working with babies (*awww*); 2) The commitment is for five sessions over the course of five weeks. We run the course once a term, which is not too much of a demand on people's time, and 3) It's really good fun doing it!

Money. Putting it bluntly: Have you got any money?

To set up Starting Rite from scratch and paying the recommended retail price for all the items required for a group of ten babies and their carers, you'll be looking at a budget of approximately £850, though this can be reduced drastically (see Chapter 3: Setting up the space).

Current baptism preparation. How will Starting Rite fit in with your current baptism preparation?

As has been mentioned, Starting Rite can be used as a baptism preparation course (though please do read Chapter 11: Taking it further), but it can also run alongside whatever you have in place already.

Where you live

Here you are trying to establish a few indicators:

- Are there enough families with babies in the area?
- Are these families likely to be church-sympathetic?
- Are these families the sort of people who will attend groups?

You can find all this out by doing a bit of research.

How many baptisms do you have a year?

If you have plenty of baptisms (say over twenty a year), then the answer
to the first two questions is a good start. Move on to the next section – 'Is
there a children's centre in your area?' If you don't have many baptisms, you
can find out whether there are families with Starting Rite-age children, by
going to: http://neighbourhood.statistics.gov.uk/HTMLDocs/Local%20Pro-
files%20V5.0/Localprofiles.html

The Church of England Research and Statistics Department has produced
a valuable resource by bringing together and publishing a range of information about each parish, both in terms of their congregations, and also
the wider community living in the area. These are called 'Parish Spotlights'
and are available to view on many diocesan websites. For example, here's
the data for Leicester diocese: www.leicester.anglican.org/shaped-by-God/
census-data/

Is there a children's centre in your area?

Try: www.gov.uk/find-sure-start-childrens-centre or google 'Sure Start
children's centres'.

If there is one, go and visit it in person. If you know someone who regularly
uses the centre, go with them. You could make an appointment to see the
manager. Take a pot-plant, smile sweetly and say, 'Is there any chance you
could give me some statistics about your Sure Start activities?' As I mention
in the Introduction, I used our local children's centre regularly, and when I
first thought about Starting Rite, I asked the receptionist for some statistics
about group sizes and attendance and also asked to survey the parents/carers
who used the facility. They were very happy about all of this. It's worth
explaining that you are intending to run a (free-of-charge) group for carers
and babies and are researching the 'market'. Find out if there are groups
specifically aimed at babies. How many attend? Are there waiting lists? This

will tell you whether the people in your area are willing and able to attend groups of this nature.

If there isn't a children's centre in your area (and there isn't in mine), then find out about other groups that run locally. These may be businesses, for example, a baby massage class, a music group or others (Jo Jingles is a well-known one). Some may be church-led mums and toddler groups. Approach them to find out the same sort of information.

Religious background

Hopefully you will more or less know the faith profile of your parish, but it may be worth finding this out as well. The 2011 census can provide some very useful information about the religious affiliation of the people in your area; go to:

www.ons.gov.uk/ons/publications/re-reference-tables.html?edition=tcm%3A77-286262

and scroll down to and click on:

2011 Census: KS209EW Religion, local authorities in England and Wales (Excel sheet 270Kb)

Working together

Working with your deanery or ecumenically

If you live in a rural area or there simply aren't many young families in your parish, it may be worth exploring the possibility of joining up with your neighbouring parishes, mission area partnerships, clusters, deanery or latest collective noun adopted by the Church of England in your diocese. Our benefice already covers seven villages but we've had carers coming in from at least four other parishes, travelling up to seven miles to attend our Starting Rite course. A further advantage of running Starting Rite as a deanery or other project is the sharing of the costs involved (see Chapter 3: Setting up the space).

But before springing this on an unsuspecting deanery synod/Churches Together group, a few things may need consideration:

- Which church has the most appropriate premises for a Starting Rite course? (See the heading 'Do you have a suitable venue?' in Chapter 2, and the heading 'Your venue' in Chapter 3.)
- Is it geographically well placed; fairly accessible by public transport or road links and situated in a central location?
- Are potential leaders or helpers able and willing to travel to another location?

Hopefully, all this gives you a flavour of Starting Rite, its background, values and mission (in all senses of the word) and whether it might work in your context. The next chapter, Chapter 2: Preparing to run your first Starting Rite course, explains all you need to know in order to set up and run a course.

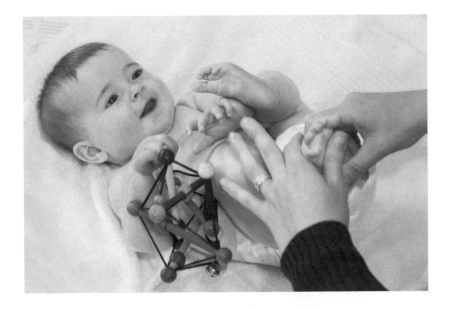

2

Preparing to run your first Starting Rite course

If you're ready to run a Starting Rite course, then it's time to think about a few practicalities. This chapter will help you work out venue, numbers, timings, childcare and advertising.

Getting started

There are four key questions for you to consider.

1. Do you have a suitable venue?

There is more detailed thinking about your venue in Chapter 3, but first and foremost please consider the following:

Size, access and facilities

Your venue needs to be:

- A *minimum* of 4 m x 5 m in size (for a group of eight participants). This is free, open floor space. If there are chairs or tables they would need to be moved elsewhere. (For smaller groups, you could use someone's living room – see numbers below and Chapter 3.)
- Heated, or be able to be heated. The ideal temperature for your room is cosy but not tropical: 18–21°C is what you are aiming for.

Your venue needs to provide:

- Pushchair/wheelchair access.
- Toilets and preferably baby-changing facilities.
- Facilities for making hot drinks (even if this means you bring mugs, tea, coffee, milk, kettle – as long as you can plug it in somewhere). The kettle is important because carers may need to warm up baby milk.
- An area for pushchairs/prams to be parked.

Ideally, your venue also needs storage for all your boxes of equipment (although you can store it elsewhere). You may also need to think about car parking space if participants are likely to be driving to the course.

2. Numbers. How many babies and caregivers are going to be in this first group?

The number you decide on will depend on these criteria:

- The space you have (is it a vicarage front room/church vestry/cavernous church hall?); try bringing a few babies and carers along and see how they all fit in a circle on the floor. Do remember that other carers, family members and godparents can be invited on the last session, so keep some space for them too or move venues.
- The numbers of families with small children in the area (see previous section).

I recommend a minimum of four babies and a maximum of ten. If you have too few, you may find on the week of a chickenpox epidemic, that you're singing lullabies to yourself. If you have too many, the piercing volume of multiple screaming babies can frankly make your eardrums bleed and the unconditional love you would hope to demonstrate for those children starts to wane rather rapidly.

I set a limit of eight babies per course; this fits our church hall facilities well. And being an introvert, I'm more comfortable with smaller rather than larger groups and I feel I get to know the families better. However, it's important to be conservatively flexible with this target, so I'll go down to five and up to ten if necessary. I've had situations where a mum and baby have showed up on the day and that's fine. Never turn people away, unless there's a very good reason: it's creating a health and safety or safeguarding problem, for example.

3. When is the best time to start our first Starting Rite course?

Time of year

First, check your baptism numbers. When is there a surge and when is it quiet? In our group of churches, we have between thirty-five and forty baptisms a year; most of these fall between the beginning of March and the end of August. The spring and summer months seem to appeal to parents, so a good time to run the first Starting Rite course would be in the run-up to the bulge in numbers. In terms of attracting numbers of carers, our experience of running eight Starting Rite courses has revealed that the autumn has so far been the least successful season to run a programme. January through to June has proved to be the best period.

Second, do you know any expectant mums through your congregation or mums and toddlers groups? This is probably the best source of babies. Word of mouth is very powerful. One mum may well invite two or three others through their own pre- or post-natal or NCT (National Childbirth Trust) groups or other networks. It may be worth waiting until a baby whose family has good contact with the church reaches about two months. Talk to the mum about whether they would be prepared to invite others. For our first Starting Rite, four of the mums already had some contact with the church; two of these invited friends and one came despite having no contact with the church except a baptism booking. Remember that for a Starting Rite course, the babies can be anything from three weeks old to one year. Carers and babies may feel too fragile if the latter is under three weeks; but once they're seriously mobile, they're too old. So bear your timing in mind when you're considering approaching a carer with a baby in hand.

Third, have consecutive sessions that avoid holidays (school and Bank).

Starting Rite runs over a period of about five weeks and contains five sessions. Make sure that the first session starts not long after the beginning of a school term or half-term and that the last session falls at least a week before the end of that half-term. It is also good to check that the last session, which is a Saturday, does not coincide with a Bank Holiday weekend. Received wisdom on running courses indicates that if you break the pattern of regular classes or meetings, you are less likely to have participants return after the break. So keep the sessions running on consecutive weeks.

Time of day

On the whole, mornings are better than afternoons in many respects. First of all, it's a good and parent-friendly routine for babies to sleep at night and be awake in the morning. Second, if the household includes pre-school or school children, then it's easy to drop the older ones off, then come along to a group which starts not long after the beginning of the school day. Once the group starts to gel, some may also think about going for lunch together afterwards. The feedback we have received from our participants certainly affirms the time we start and finish: 9.30 am, doors open for tea and coffee, sessions run from 10 am to 11.30 am. You will find that groups vary enormously as to when they do actually roll up. We had one large group who started rocking up at 9.20 am and the next group never crossed the threshold until 10.01 am.

4. Can you offer childcare for older siblings?

If you can, you will attract more carers and babies. The feedback we've received from carers of more than one child often highlights the value and appreciation of some quality and exclusive time with their youngest. So it makes lots of sense to run Starting Rite on a weekday morning during term-time (when school-age siblings are in class), but you may well have caregivers who need some provision for a pre-school sibling.

So if your answer is 'yes, we can' you need to ensure that you can close off from the toddlers the space in which the Starting Rite group will be meeting. The engine noises of tractors and fire-engine sirens can penetrate rather harshly the peaceful and serene atmosphere you want to create in the Starting Rite sessions. You will also need two other helpers who are good with pre-schoolers. If you already run a mums and toddlers group, the toys and activities from that are perfectly sufficient.

If it's 'no, we just can't' and you feel it's impossible to offer childcare for older ones, find out about local provision for this age-group. The government currently offers fifteen hours of free nursery or playgroup places per week for any child over the age of three.[28] If your local pre-school nursery/ group is full to bursting on a Wednesday morning, that might be the best day to run your Starting Rite course.

Advertising and getting people to come

Once you've established the answers to the above, you can start the advertisement process.

Here are a few suggestions:

- As mentioned above, the best way of recruiting is through personal contact; church toddler groups are a perfect start, if you run one.
- Ask those contacts to let others know about Starting Rite; give them fliers to hand out. (See the example on the accompanying CD.)
- You could also visit, taking fliers with you (with permission from church leaders), other church-run mums and toddlers groups in your area. Be prepared to speak clearly about who Starting Rite is for and what it's about. Expressions such as 'you might be thinking of having your baby christened' make it clear that it is about the Christian faith; it's important that people know it is 'religious' in some way.
- Make sure all your baptism families, who have babies in the 0–1 age range, are told about Starting Rite on their first point of contact with the church. Follow this up with a second phone call from the Starting Rite leader who can explain the course a bit further.
- Get in contact with your local health visitor(s). They can be marvellous at helping to promote Starting Rite, especially once they see what it does and how it's run.
- Go back to your children's centre. Remember their aim is to 'deliver the best start in life for every child by bringing together early education, childcare, health and family support'. They are also commissioned to work with and alongside the local community. You are not competing with their own health and education courses, because of the focus on the Christian faith, but you are encouraging practices they would promote, singing songs, reading books and peer support, for example. So all in all, they ought to be falling over themselves to advertise your Starting Rite for you!

---

28 Check out www.gov.uk/free-early-education for the most up-to-date information about this.

- Use local magazines, newspapers, publications, Facebook and websites, such as www.netmums.com/local-to-you, to advertise. This can be costly, but for the first launch of Starting Rite in your area it might be worth it.
- If your church has a festival – flower, Christmas tree, bake-off, and so on – make sure there's a Starting Rite entry. I do a Starting Rite Christmas tree at our Christmas tree festival; it's great for advertising and for reconnecting with families we've already met and new ones.
- Mention childcare for older ones, if you can offer it.
- Remember to make it clear in all communication that Starting Rite is free of charge!

Administration and making it work

Once you have established your maximum baby capacity, make sure you book on a first come, first served basis. Keep a record of the following:

- The carers' and babies' names; first and surnames. Make sure you understand the relationship between the carer and the baby and that you obtain an email address and telephone number for contact purposes.
- Whether they are a baptism candidate.
- How they heard about Starting Rite.
- If there are any siblings (if yes, take their names). See the enrolment table on the accompanying CD.

It's worth checking that email addresses work, because you will be contacting participants a few days before the beginning of each course, so send an email and ask them to acknowledge receipt. When you start the course, double check all these details with the participants. Let them know that the information is kept for your purposes only; you won't share it with others. Assure them that you will only use the mobile number to call them in case a session has to be cancelled at the last minute. Once the course is finished, ask participants if they are interested in staying in touch. If the answer is a firm 'no', then delete their contact details from your computer simply for data protection purposes. If they say 'yes', then you can obviously keep their details for when you are advertising other church events or activities. On the evaluation forms[29] there is a question about whether they would be interested in hearing from the church in future.

---

29 These are on the accompanying CD.

Do not be discouraged if a week before the course is due to start you only have four babies, and you were hoping for eight. In my experience, they can come along thick and fast just before the start date. And it's always good to pray.

3

Setting up the space: the venue and equipment

This section will help you prepare your premises for the Starting Rite course. It includes some health and safety advice and lists the resources you need to start.

Your venue

The room itself

Go into your venue and think about the 'feel' of it:

- Is it cavernous or intimate?
- Is it friendly looking?
- Is it well lit?

There are ways to improve the atmosphere of a hall:

- Remove clutter and store it elsewhere.
- Use carpets and screens to establish 'your area', preferably near a window for natural light.
- Use cushions around the walls to give a sense of cosiness.
- Make it warm.

If you have a small group, consider using someone's house, where there is a large room (with the owner's permission of course!). This has several advantages:

- Hopefully, it can be easily heated.
- It has a kitchen.
- It has a toilet.
- It has seats and cushions available.
- It may well have a carpet on the floor already.

However, you would need to think through where to hold the third session, Splash!, as this involves water. You would also have to bring the resources every week and take them away, unless the owner is happy to store them for you.

For all venues, you need to do a health and safety check; see below.

The floor

Go into the hall or space you will use for your Starting Rite. Lie down on your tummy and look at the floor.

- Is it clean?
- Is it warm?
- Would a hormonally enhanced mum be prepared to put her baby on it?

If the answer to any or all of the above is 'not really', then you might want to borrow or buy a carpet. The maxim here is the floor is your friend. Starting Rite groups all take place on the floor. You can't put babies on tables and they tend to slide off laps, especially when you're doing baby massage and they're all slippery. They are much safer on the floor, as long as this is clean and protected from cold and draughts.

Carers with special needs

If you have a caregiver who is not able to sit on a floor, ask them what kind of seating would work for them. We have used beanbags in the past; baby could still be on the floor with others. If you have a parent in a wheelchair, talk to them about how they change their child's nappy at home. In the Starting Rite course the physical position of parent to child is very similar to the interaction when changing nappies or clothes. You may need to acquire a changing station or trolley – ask carers with slightly older children. People often have nursery furniture stored in lofts, garages and cupboards under the stairs.

General health and safety

A thorough risk-assessment should be carried out in your venue. A basic, but not exhaustive, checklist for childproofing includes ensuring that:

- Hot radiators/water pipes are fenced off.
- Plug sockets are covered.
- Any small, swallowable objects are put out of reach.
- Sharp corners are cushioned.
- Low-level drawers/cupboards are put on childproof catches.
- Doors are wedged.
- Stairs are blocked or gated.
- The kitchen (if there is one) is off-limits (just in case there are mobile older siblings around).

It is a good plan to invite your local health visitor to come and check out your premises. They will give you advice and, where necessary, point you towards the child safety equipment required. If you ask a few parents, they may be happy to pass on some childproofing items to you (make sure they are not damaged or faulty). If not, the main supermarkets do a range of baby safety devices at reasonable prices.

Room temperature

As noted in Chapter 2, the ideal temperature for your room is 18–21°C. Some of the sessions involve stripping all baby's clothes off, so do ask the caregivers if they feel the temperature of the room is appropriate. Exclude all draughts (an alternative use for hassocks and altar kneelers?).

Comfort levels

Babies spend most of their lives cushioned – in cots, car-seats, prams, baby rockers and on carpets. So it's important to show we recognize this in what we provide for them.

Changing mats

Starting Rite provides padded changing mats for the baby to lie on during the sessions and we suggest that carers bring a soft towel for them. This ensures that the babies are on something clean (at least at the start of the session) and comfortable.

At the end of every session, you should wipe down every changing mat with a hygienic wipe.

Cushions

It's nice for carers to sit on something other than a cold, lino floor, so think about cushions, mats or beanbags for them. We use carpet samples.

Armchair or sofa?

It is also good to ensure there is somewhere for carers to feed their babies but still remain in the room with the others. A comfortable armchair or sofa is ideal, but even if they are still on the floor, they often prefer to lean up against something solid to support their backs while breastfeeding.

Equipment and storage

Although you will only physically set up your space after you have booked in your group of carers and gurgling babies, you need to prepare for this well in advance, so about *three to six months* before you plan to start your first Starting Rite course, begin the process of gathering the resources.

In this section, you will find out about the costs involved and tips on keeping these to a minimum. There are lists of the equipment and ideas on where to get it from and how to organize the items into boxes for each session.

How much does Starting Rite cost?

It is a truth universally acknowledged that a single baby born tiny and naked into the world must be in want of a disproportionate amount of gear. Travel cots, changing stations, baby baths, car seats, travel systems, rocking chairs, pushchairs, highchairs, swing chairs, moses baskets and buggies; that's just off the top of my head and all of these are simply to move, eat, wash and sleep. This list doesn't even touch on anything to play with.

Starting Rite does mirror to an extent the quantities of goods needed for these little ones. There is a lot of storage required and the equipment does cost; please be prepared for this. We are not talking about spending a tenner on some craft materials.

If you buy all the equipment new, you're looking at spending about £850, but before you baulk and lob this book into your recycling, there are ways of reducing these costs, and remember Starting Rite materials can be used again and again, and can be shared with other churches.

Start early

The top tip on reducing costs is to start hunting and gathering the goodies as soon as possible, hence the tip on starting three to six months beforehand. Be on the look-out for bargains and discounts and keep asking others if they could lend you any of it on a permanent basis. Every time I run a Starting Rite course, I have to ask one mum to lend me a book just for one session; I can't get hold of the book any other way – it's out of print[30] – but she's always ready to lend it and that's really helpful.

It took me about two years to get together everything I wanted; this is because I was literally making it up as I went along; you should only need three to six months. I cannot emphasize enough how advantageous it is to

---

30 Just to reassure you, all the books recommended for the first three sessions are in print. When I started the course, I used this particular book, which unfortunately went out of print shortly afterwards.

start early because you might find that all of a sudden the book *Guess How Much I Love You* is on at a bargain price of £2.50 instead of £4.99 in Babies R Us for the week following the third Sunday before Lent; and when you need nine copies of it, it's really worth braving ice and wind to get your thermally lined mittens on them.

Essential and optional items

There are things you really have to have for the Starting Rite course and there are optional extras. I have marked where things are optional; here you can either leave it out altogether or find something that will work instead.

New and second-hand

Much of the equipment can be bought second-hand. You can try websites like eBay and Amazon for some of the books and hardware. However, there are resources that must be bought new for health and safety reasons. Some of the items on the list below are marked with an asterisk *; these should all be purchased brand new.

Read the rest of this book

It's worth reading about how you are going to use the equipment. Sometimes I give a brief indication about what the item will be used for in the list below, but it would be impossible to explain this in detail for every object. There are cost-saving reasons for reading the rest of this book before going on a spending spree. You'll have a much better understanding of the purpose of each item.

- You won't end up buying something and then realizing it's not quite fit for purpose.
- You or your church community might already have something that will work instead or even better.
- You might want to use a different story in Storytime and therefore buy alternative props.

What do you need for a Starting Rite course?

As there is an awful lot of stuff to collect, I have first of all grouped the items under headings, which hopefully will help you as you shop for them. Later in this chapter the items are grouped under the sessions for which they are needed.

The quantity required assumes you are running a course for eight babies. (Nine is given under the heading 'quantity' just in case an extra mum and baby turn up unexpectedly, and remember, when reading the books, you need a copy too, which is why the number ten is given for books!)

Books

You can buy the books second-hand, but they must be in good condition. Children's books can get ripped, marked and bitten! Do also shop around. Try:

- Marks & Spencer – they do sell baby books sometimes at reduced prices
- www.amazon.co.uk is always good especially for second-hand
- www.bookdepository.co.uk/
- The Works
- Mothercare
- Boots
- Early Learning Centre
- Major supermarkets.

Item	Quantity	Cost (new)	Notes
Peekaboo Baby! by Mandy Ross, illustrated by Kate Merritt (Ladybird)	10	£6.99	There are flaps in this book; if buying second-hand make sure they're not ripped
Some other *Peekaboo* books: e.g. *Baby Faces Peekaboo!* (Dorling Kindersley); *Eyes, Nose, Toes Peekaboo!* (Dorling Kindersley)	1 of each	About £6 each	These are optional; just to have around the middle of the room for carers to pick up and read to their babies. You only need 1 copy of each and 2 or 3 is plenty
Guess How Much I Love You board book by Sam McBratney, illustrated by Anita Jeram (Walker Books)	10	£4.99	This is the normal size (16 x 14 cm) board book
Guess How Much I Love You snuggle book by Sam McBratney, illustrated by Anita Jeram (Walker Books)	1	£10	This is optional. It is useful in case you have a really tiny (under two months-old) baby
I Love You by Giles Andreae, illustrated by Emma Dodd	1	£6.99	This is optional; again for carers to read as and when to their baby
God Knows All About Me board book by Claire Page (Authentic Media)	10	£5.99	You need to search for the revised edition; ISBN 9781860249501

Item	Quantity	Cost (new)	Notes
Art for Baby, various (Templar Publishing)	1	£14.99	This is optional. The book contains various highly contrasting pictures suitable for very young babies. Some of the book price goes towards the NSPCC
Some other books that talk about bubbles: e.g. *Bubble Trouble* board book by Margaret Mahy, illustrated by Polly Dunbar	1	£4.98	These are optional for carers to look at with their babies
A whole range of children's Bibles, particularly the ones recommended on the Storytime handout	around 20	Vary from £4.99 to £15 each	You could try asking your local Christian bookshop (if you have one) to do a sale or return for the Storytime session. This will save you buying them all, or you could try and do a deal with the bookshop

Items that can be sourced from charity shops/table top sales/car boots/your loft

As these can be second-hand, their condition does not need to be pristine, but all items must be clean and safe for a baby to handle. Damaged items cannot be used.

I haven't costed this, because you're looking for as low a price as possible! If you can't find them in charity shops, then you will have to buy them new, unless they are marked as optional.

Item	Quantity	Notes
Various toy balls; of different colours, sizes and textures	About 25	They need to be reasonably light and the smallest must be equal to or bigger than the size of a satsuma
Pillow or large cushion	1	
Soft toy sheep, all different shapes, colours, sizes and textures	Minimum of 10	As many as possible
Small plastic funnels	1 or 2	These are for filling up the travel-size plastic bottles with baby oil. You can also get them from supermarkets
Plastic toy shells	1 or 2	Optional
CD of children's/babies' music	1	But any child-friendly music will do
Large plastic jug	1	This is to scoop up sand and needs to be sturdy
Decent rug or thick blanket approx. 250 x 150cm, preferably colourful and patterned	1	As this may not be easy to find second-hand, this item is also listed under Furnishings on p. 58

Stationery

Try: Staples, the Range, Office Direct, WH Smith, supermarkets, craft shops.

Item	Quantity	Cost	Notes
Sticky or post-it notes:* different shapes and colours	5 blocks of notes	Between £2.99 and £5 per pack	
Biros	10		
Marker pens	3		
Thin card, i.e. 160 gsm	9 sheets		
Mirror card, different colours	25 sheets of A4	£3.50 for pack of 10 sheets	This card has a metallic reflective surface; try to get at least 10 silver-coloured cards and then others of different colours, but they must all be reflective

Baby items

Most of these (marked with an *) must be bought new for reasons of hygiene and professionalism. Try: supermarkets, large chemists, and other baby stores, for example, Boots, Mothercare, Babies R Us.

Item	Quantity	Cost	Notes
Changing mats.* Padded PVC mat with soft, slightly raised side walls	9	Between £5 and £10 each	
Tissues*	2 boxes	Cheapest is fine	
Roll of kitchen paper*	1	Cheapest is fine	
Baby wipes*	2 packets	Between £1 and £2 per packet	'Sensitive skin' best
Antibacterial surface wipes* (e.g. Milton or Dettol)	1 packet	Between £1.50 and £3 per packet	To wipe down changing mats after each session
Room thermometer	1	Between £5 and £15	If you speak very nicely to your local health visitor, they might give you one
Bath thermometer	1	Between £3.99 and £10	You can get a bath and room thermometer combined – these cost about £17, but again try health visitors

Item	Quantity	Cost	Notes
Baby sponges* – different shapes and colours	4 or 5	Between 50p and £5	
Screw top travel bottles (100 ml)	9	About £1.50	Need to be clean if not new
Large bottle of baby oil	1	Between £4–£5	

Hardware/outdoor items

Try places like: B&Q, Homebase, Wickes, www.amazon.co.uk, www.ebay.co.uk/

Item	Quantity	Cost	Notes
Blackout or sensory tent/pod/den	1	£60–£100	Try: SensaHut – Sensory Blackout Tent – Pop Up – £99 Giant Dark Den – £66.99 Alternatively, try using a cheap 3–4-person tent and have someone sew a cover for it using blackout material. Try: GO Outdoors Bondi 4 Person Tent – £35
Cement mixer trays	2	£18–£20	It's useful to have two: one that has a large open surface area (approx. 1 m in diameter), with low (around 6 cm) sides (try Tuffspot Mixing Tray); one with higher (around 8 cm) sides (e.g. Homebase)

Item	Quantity	Cost	Notes
Large piece of tarpaulin (2 m x 3 m)	1	Around £5–£8	For spillages in Splash!
Quantity of pebbles or cobblestones	about 40	Around £8–£10 for a large bag	You can pick these off a beach or river bank, but they must be smooth-ish; no sharp edges and, in size, equal to or larger than a satsuma
Play sand	1 bag (15 kg)	£3	This must be **play sand**; builders' sand stains skin and clothes

Material/fabric

For the material, it's worth going to markets. If you travel during the months you're looking out for Starting Rite provisions, get yourself down to a local market; there's bound to be something cheap and fascinating from a baby's point of view. The look on one baby's face when presented with a piece of sparkly orange chiffon was 'Wow! This stuff is awesome!'

You are looking for odd cuts and end of reels, so this should reduce the price. Look in remnant bins, and negotiate with market traders.

It is difficult to give prices for this. One remnant piece of really beautiful shot silk with lovely colours and textures might be worth paying a bit more for, whereas a piece of white netting might be 25p.

Instead I've put which session the pieces are for: if you read the chapter on that session, it might give you an idea of what type and size material would work best.

There's also no harm in asking around friends and relations. Most people have off-cuts or material they 'just kept'.

Avoid big department stores, unless they're offering really good reductions. Otherwise they're very expensive.

Item	Quantity	Session	Notes
Large piece of blue(ish) material (preferably Lycra or voile)	1	Bubble-Talk and Storytime	Ours is 3 m x 4 m; this is pretty big. 2 m x 3 m would be OK. You may have to sew 2 pieces together
Lots of pieces of red material	At least 6	Peek-a-Boo! and Storytime	Long scarves will do (light, chiffony material, not knitted). This is for the story of the Exodus
Lots of pieces of grey material	At least 6	Peek-a-Boo! and Storytime	Long scarves will do (light, chiffony material, not knitted) This is for the story of the Exodus
Material printed with farm animals on it	1	Peek-a-Boo! and Storytime	Farm animals print is best; but other animals will be OK: bees, birds. This is for the story of the Lost Sheep. Between 0.5 and 1 m
Piece of green material	1	Storytime	This is for the story of the Lost Sheep. About 1 m
Pieces of other material of all textures, colours, designs, patterns and different degrees of transparency	About 10–15 pieces	Peek-a-Boo!	It's useful for some of the material to be semi-see-through, e.g. voiles or netting. Between 0.5 and 1 m. Avoid buttons, loose sequins and tassels – these may be bitten off by babies and swallowed

Furnishings

These items can be expensive. Shop around. If you need a large carpet, try an end of roll at a carpet shop. Your carpet does not need to fit a room perfectly, but it does need to be rolled up and put away somewhere afterwards, so make sure you have storage and can lift it! Try: IKEA, Argos, CarpetRight, www.amazon.co.uk, Wilco, B&Q.

Item	Quantity	Cost	Notes
Seat pads or hassocks or carpet samples	9	About £3–£5 each	Discontinued lines of carpet may mean a shop is throwing out samples
If cold, unwelcoming floor: decent carpet. Either 4 m x 5 m or combination of rugs	1	About £5–£15 per metre	If you do feel the need for a very large carpet, you do not need to buy the rug below, just a patterned blanket would be sufficient
Decent rug or thick blanket approx 250 x 150 cm, preferably colourful and patterned	1	About £60–£80	IKEA, Helsinge rug: 230 x 160 cm – £55 Argos, Maestro Floral Rug: 230 x 160 cm – £69.99
Cushions – any	3 or 4	£7.50	These are optional, depending on your venue and whether extra comfort would be advisable. These do not need to be new; just clean

Miscellaneous

Item	Quantity	From	Cost	Notes
Baby Massage posters*	5	www.babymassageposter.com/	£8.95 each	Buy a group set of 4 for £29.95 plus one single for £8.95
Towels	3	Your linen cupboard!		Spares for carers who forget to bring one
Electric tealights*	10	www.amazon.co.uk Daffodil LEC006 – LED tealights – electric flameless candles with holders – at the time of writing, it was not clear whether the holder was made of plastic or glass	£7 for pack of 6	You can buy others, but make sure they can be chewed! Holders must be plastic
Bottles of bubble mixture*	9	Major supermarkets, Wilko, the Range, Early Learning Centre	£3 to £4 for pack of 6	Mini bottles are fine or make your own
Large beach ball	1	www.amazon.co.uk Splash and Play giant inflatable beach ball 48"	£15	This is optional

Item	Quantity	From	Cost	Notes
Small beach balls	3 or 4	www.amazon.co.uk Bestway Splash Designer Splat 16" swimming pool beach ball	£2.50 each	
Moses	1	Try searching the Internet. You need a 30 cm/12" tall doll that looks like Moses; i.e. old, bearded, dressed in Ancient Near East-style clothing and carrying a staff. Alternatively ask if there is someone in your congregation who can knit a Moses character of similar dimensions and dress. If all else fails, dress up a large doll in a robe.		

Starting Rite resources

These are all on the accompanying CD. They are available to print off, but some need to be laminated; see Notes column.

Item	Quantity	From	Cost	Notes
Song Books	11	On the accompanying CD		9 copies for participants and 2 for leaders. Laminate and bind them
Handouts	9 of each for every course	On the accompanying CD		These are given to participants, so you have to keep printing new copies for each course. Laminate
Evaluation forms	9	On the accompanying CD		These are given to participants, so you have to keep printing new copies for each course
'Speak to me in bubbles'	10	On the accompanying CD		9 copies for participants and 1 for leaders. Follow the instructions (also on the CD) on how to produce these. You will need to print, slice, laminate and bind them; give yourself time to do this

Just a note concerning the items on the CD. The handouts, Song Books and the 'Speak to me in bubbles' book do contain copyrighted materials. In purchasing the book, permission is granted for photocopies to be made for use in Starting Rite sessions only.

Lamination, lamination, lamination

> Out of the mouths of infants and nursing babies
> you have prepared praise for yourself

… but also quite a lot of regurgitated milk for their mums. And that is why we laminate.

Photos and music

If you plan to take photos you will also need a camera or a device that can take photos (iPad/iPhone) and you will need a CD player or other contraption that plays music.

Storing the equipment

Because you use equipment over and over again, you need to protect it from theft, damp, creepy-crawlies and other things that came about after The Fall. Large 45-litre storage boxes with lids seem to work well at keeping all the necessaries together. Do remember they will need to be stored somewhere appropriate. You need eight storage boxes altogether.

The boxes and what they contain

The list of equipment is divided up into boxes. (We are carrying on with the assumption you have eight participants on your course.) After each item, the relevant table of where to source the object is noted in brackets. The eight boxes are:

Box named 'Set-Up'

Ideally this box should be kept on the premises for the duration of the Starting Rite course, because you need it every week. It includes all the items needed to set up for every session.

- 10 biro pens (Stationery)
- 2 boxes of tissues (Baby items)
- 5 blocks of post-its (Stationery)
- 2 packets of baby wipes (Baby items)
- 9 carpet mats (Furnishings)
- 1 roll of kitchen paper (Baby items)
- 1 packet of antibacterial wipes (Baby items)
- 1 room thermometer (Baby items)
- 1 decent rug or thick blanket (Furnishings)
- 9 name cards – fold a piece of A4 card in half to make A5, then fold again in a way that makes a long thin strip (not A6 postcard size), sellotape the two end flaps on top of each other to make a 'Toblerone' shape. Write the name of the baby underlined and then his or her carer's name or allow carer to do it (hence need for marker pens).
- Marker pens (Stationery)
- 11 Starting Rite Song Books (CD)
- List of participants
- Leader's folder
- Door signs
- Camera
- *9 changing mats (Baby items)*
- *If cold floor: decent carpet/rug; either 4 m x 5 m or combination of rugs (Furnishings)*

The last two items will not fit into the box but are also used in every session.

Box named 'Peek-a-Boo!'

- 10 copies of *Peekaboo Baby!* by Mandy Ross (Books)
- Mirror cards (Stationery)
- Lots of different material (about 15–20 different pieces) (Material/fabric)
- Other *Peekaboo* books, e.g. *Baby Faces Peekaboo!* (Dorling Kindersley), *Eyes, Nose, Toes Peekaboo!* (Dorling Kindersley) (Books)
- Handouts (CD)

Box named 'How Much Love?'

- 10 copies of *Guess How Much I Love You* board book by Sam McBratney (Books)
- 1 copy of *Guess How Much I Love You* soft cloth book (Books)
- 1 copy of *I Love You* by Giles Andreae (Books)
- 5 Baby Massage posters (Miscellaneous)
- 9 small plastic travel bottles (Baby items)
- 1 large bottle of baby oil (Baby items)
- Funnels (Charity shops/your loft)
- Handouts (CD)

Box named 'Splash!'

- 10 copies of *God Knows All About Me* by Claire Page (Books)
- NSPCC *Art for Baby* book (Books)
- Tarpaulin (Hardware/outdoor items)
- Bath thermometer (Baby items)
- Towels (Miscellaneous)
- Sponges (Baby items)
- Electric tealights (Miscellaneous)
- Plastic scallop-shaped shell (Charity shops/your loft)
- Handouts (CD)
- *Blackout tent/sensory den (Hardware/outdoor items)*
- *Cement mixer trays (Hardware/outdoor items)*

The last two items will not fit into the box, but are also part of this session.

Box named 'Bubble-Talk Box 1'

- 10 copies of 'Speak to me in bubbles' by Jenny Paddison (CD)
- 'Bubble' books (Books)
- Large piece of blue material (Material/fabric)
- 9 bottles bubble mixture (Miscellaneous)
- CD of children's music (Charity shops/your loft)
- CD player (Your home/church)

Box named 'Bubble-Talk Box 2'

- Various toy balls (Charity shops/your loft)
- 1 large beach ball (Miscellaneous)
- Small beach balls (Miscellaneous)
- Handouts (CD)

Box named 'Storytime Box 1'

- Large cushion or pillow (Charity shops/your loft or Furnishings or your home)
- Pieces of farm animal and green material (Material/fabric)
- Toy sheep (Charity shops/your loft)
- Pebbles (Hardware/outdoor items)
- Plastic jug (Charity shops/your loft/your home)

Box named 'Storytime Box 2'

- Red and grey material (Material/fabric)
- Large blue material (Material/fabric)
- 'Moses'/shepherd doll (Miscellaneous)
- Range of children's Bible stories (Books)
- Handouts (CD)
- Feedback forms
- *Large bag of play sand (Hardware/outdoor items)*
- *Cement mixer trays (Hardware/outdoor items)*

The last two items will not fit into the box, but are also part of this session.

Getting your boxes organized

Printing out labels with the list of equipment for each box is A Good Thing; this makes it easier to ensure you have everything before the sessions. It also means that when you have a few people packing away, they know exactly which items to put in the correct box. On the accompanying CD, there is a document – 'labels for SR storage boxes' – with all the labels required for the boxes. Print on large addressing labels (99.1 x 139 mm) – one A4 sheet will contain 4 labels.

It is good to gather everything before the beginning of the course; clearly you need everything for the 'Set-Up box' and the Peek-a-Boo! box, but if you haven't managed to get the odd item for later sessions, it's not the end of the world. For example, bubble mixture is not needed until the fourth session (Bubble-Talk) so you have got three weeks and you can probably pick it up at your next supermarket run.

Hospitality

Most church events provide tea, coffee and biscuits and Starting Rite is no different. In fact, it's really important; these caregivers are on call 24/7 to provide unstintingly for others' needs. So when you offer them a cup of tea and a chocolate brownie, you may be surprised at the seemingly disproportionate amount of appreciation they demonstrate. It is best if another helper (not the Starting Rite leader) offers the hospitality, as this gives you a chance to concentrate on the carers and babies themselves.

Information for course participants

In the week leading up to the first session, send out an email to all the caregivers. Make sure the email is sent to recipients in *blind copy*; this is because of confidentiality – people might not like the idea of their email address advertised to strangers. You can send an email blind copy by clicking on your 'cc' button at the top of an email you are about to send. The box that comes up on your screen will give you the option to place all your email addresses in the 'Bcc' box, which is blind copy. This ensures that no one receiving the email can see the addresses of the other recipients.

The email should include the following information:

- An attachment of the 'initial handout' (see accompanying CD) plus a sentence indicating its presence within the email!
- A reminder of when and where the course starts.
- Ask them to bring a towel for their baby and a baby record book that they may or may not have started filling in. (These come in all shapes and sizes, but generally ask the same questions: 'When did your baby first smile/sit up/clap/puke/compose a critically acclaimed clarinet concerto?') The purpose of bringing the book becomes clear under each session.
- Clear instructions about when a baby should not attend a session. It should run something like this: 'Please consider carefully whether it's wise to bring your baby to a session if they are poorly. If your baby has a temperature, an upset tummy or an infectious illness, such as chickenpox, indeed if you are in any doubt about their state of health, please contact your GP and stay at home for that week.'

On this note of baby health, please remember that you are not a professional medical expert. Parents do look for advice and guidance from leaders of baby groups, but please don't ever give advice about diagnosing or treating illness or any other physical health concern a parent might have. Other carers in the group might suggest treatments, for example, a different nappy rash cream, and that's fine, but the best approach for you is to direct them to their health visitor or GP.

Setting up and putting away

Give yourself plenty of time to set up the sessions each week. You probably need to arrive at least an hour beforehand, especially if you're on your own and it's the first time you've done this. The first time I ran the Bubble-Talk session, it took me half an hour to blow up one (admittedly giant) beach ball. If your venue is free the evening beforehand, you might prefer to set it up at that point so you're ready in the morning. Be aware that some of the setting up involves heavy lifting, so involve others if you can. It's good to set up and give yourself time for a cup of tea and a prayer before they all arrive. It also takes about an hour to put everything away again.

Praying for your families

Once you've got a list of caregivers and babies, do start praying for them and encourage your church to do likewise. If you know them, you might be aware of some pastoral needs, and as you get to know the others, they may well share some of their lives with you. Another area of prayer is that the parents will start praying themselves. There is a short time of reflection about prayer in the Starting Rite course every week to encourage the adults to do some at home. In short, pray for parental prayer. Finally pray for yourself and other helpers. Starting Rite is a commitment of time, leadership, mission and ministry; ask God to strengthen and guide you through this. During one of our Starting Rite courses, all the leaders were going through a tough time in one way or another and our prayers were mostly dedicated towards supporting each other. At the end of the course, without knowing what we were going through, the mums had clubbed together and bought each of us a bunch of flowers!

We're now going to move on to the sessions themselves, some theological reflection about them and some practical advice.

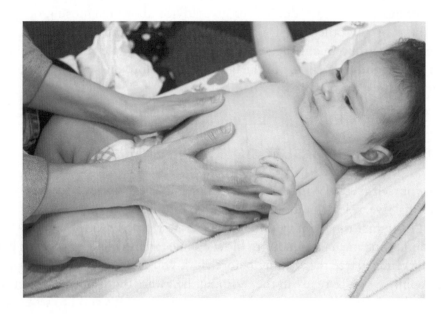

4

An overview of the Starting Rite sessions

In this chapter, we're going to look at the choice and order of the sessions, so let's start by reminding ourselves of the five sessions and the Christian topics they explore:

1. Peek-a-Boo! – The mystery of God
2. How Much Love? – God's unconditional love
3. Splash! – Baptism symbolism
4. Bubble-Talk – Prayer
5. Storytime – Scripture

I wrestled long and hard with these topics. Can you really tackle the mystery of God with a handful of cute but inarticulate small mammals? And does the order matter? Should Splash! be first, or should we lead up to it as the culmination of the course, if we're meeting with baptism families? Couldn't we swap over Bubble-Talk and Storytime?

Now I've run the course a number of times, I've settled on the topics and the order listed above. The reason for this is because at the heart of Starting Rite is relationship building. During the course relationships are being encouraged and nurtured: the relationship between carer and baby; the relationship between baby and other babies; the relationship between carer and other carers; and the relationship between participating families and the church community. But the one that gives sense and meaning to all the above is the relationship between us and God.

Stories of relationships

The course implicitly follows the story of two mirroring relationships over a course of time: the relationship between a carer and his/her child and the relationship of a person coming to faith in God. The table below tracks, in the first column, the developing relationship between a mother and a child; the quotes are taken from a psychologist's summary of this mutual attachment. The middle column follows the corresponding stages of someone coming to faith in God. This is not a universal representation of how people experience conversion to Christianity but is not untypical of testimony stories. The last column notes the Starting Rite session that aims to reflect that stage of the relationship.

Mother and baby[31]	Person and God	Starting Rite session
'During the first year of life, infants are social beings whose sensory systems focus on interacting with the primary caregivers.'	A person begins to be aware of God, of a transcendental presence, in ways that invite him or her into relationship.	Peek-a-Boo!
'During such interactions, [sometimes] called "attunement" (the sharing of affect between mother and infant), the infant's brain is stimulated, positive emotions of interest and joy develop and the child begins to feel special.'	The person becomes aware of God's love and can trust in God; the more he or she trusts, the more they understand God's love for them.	How Much Love?

---

31 'The Development of Attachment, Normal Developmental Attachment': http://www.fatih.edu.tr/~hugur/Friendly/Adopting%20Children%20with.PDF, Daniel A. Hughes.

Starting Rite session	Person and God	Starting Rite session
'In contrast to the first year, when the mother teaches her infant that he is special, during the second year ... she actively socializes her child by saying "no", channeling his behaviors, setting limits and not responding to all of his wishes. When she frustrates her child's wishes, he feels shame ... This experience of shame causes emotional distress, which the mother intuitively recognizes. She reattunes with her child with a smile, touch, or supportive word and reassures him that he is special but also that he must be aware of the rights and feelings of others. Within moments, the toddler feels special again.'	The person has a sense of their own limitations and imperfections vis-à-vis God, but once this realization is acknowledged (or confessed) God allows for a fresh start, because he offers grace and forgiveness.	Splash!
'The young child, within the safety of this secure attachment, learns to integrate both attunement and shame as well as his own wishes and the demands of socialization. He learns how to remain close to his mother ... he learns to integrate and accept the "good" and "bad" parts of himself .... The child develops the ability to consistently ... control his behaviors, and recognize the difference between right and wrong .... As he "downloads" his parents' love into his developing self, he trusts that they will do what is best for him and will keep him safe.'	The person pursues the relationship with God through repeated encounter with him in worship: prayer and Scripture. This has an ongoing transformative effect on his or her life for the good.	Bubble-Talk and Storytime

The topics

Let's now take a closer look at the topics themselves and how each one ties in with the stages outlined above.

Peek-a-Boo! – appreciating the mystery of God

People feel uncomfortable talking about God; he is one of the few taboo subjects left in our society. In their research into children's spirituality, David Hay and Rebecca Nye noted that during Rebecca's interviews with the children:

> Some children admitted that they were afraid of being laughed at or thought stupid or even mad, not only by their peer group but also within their families (including 'religious' families), if they talk about their personal sense of the religious in their lives.[32]

We have to acknowledge this sense of embarrassment but also help people get over it in a Starting Rite course. The message is: God is with us; let's get used to it! The focus of the course is our relationship with God: it's *kinda* difficult to explore this without mentioning him from the start.

One of the reasons people feel uncomfortable is because of the mystery of God; having a faith involves accepting something that we can't fully comprehend. Adults are wary of things they don't understand.

So Session 1, Peek-a-Boo!, is there right at the start because it squares up to this issue and tackles it face to face. This session and its handout recognizes the mystery of God and examines how we can begin to sense God in our lives in a way that allows some understanding of him. Indeed, these cute, inarticulate babes rank among the most receptive created beings around to appreciate the glory, the awe and the majesty that make up the mystery of God.

---

32 David Hay with Rebecca Nye, *The Spirit of the Child*, revd edn, London: Jessica Kingsley, 2006, p. 103.

The main aim of Peek-a-Boo! is:

- to evoke our awareness of God.

Other aims:

- to acknowledge that this awareness is difficult to articulate

- to promote the idea that mystery can be welcomed; that mystery can invite, not repel, trust in God

- to overthrow the taboo of talking about God.

How Much Love? – trust and love

Session 2, How Much Love?, encourages the beginnings of trust. Its focus is on the unconditional love of God. The Bible begins with a relationship between God and humanity that was based on mutual and unconditional trust, and such loving and open trust allowed for the vulnerability of nakedness. Babies are born naked and vulnerable; this nakedness expects a loving response that, if forthcoming, establishes trust in the child. How Much Love? involves baby touch. This touch, like massage, takes babies back to nakedness; but the act of massage is a demonstration of the carer's desire to bond with their child and encourages the further growth of trust.

The main aim of How Much Love? is:

- to invite people into a knowledge of God's unboundaried love for us.

We do this by:

- establishing that God's nature is loving

- reassuring that we can trust God, because of his love for us

- wondering about the extent of God's love.

Splash! – baptism: an intentional return towards God

This session carries on the story of our relationship with God. Here we acknowledge that this perfect, loving and trusting relationship fails at times. There is a recognition that we can and will do things wrong. It introduces implicitly the concept of free will; in the act of baptism we choose to return to relationship with God in The Decision:

The president addresses the candidates directly, or through their parents, godparents and sponsors

Therefore I ask:
Do you turn to Christ?
I turn to Christ.

Do you repent of your sins?
I repent of my sins.

Do you renounce evil?
I renounce evil.

Splash! takes centre stage in the Starting Rite course, the third of a five-session course, but this position makes it clear that baptism is a landmark stage on an *ongoing* journey. It doesn't just stop at baptism; the journey continues in company with God through prayer and his word.

The main aim of Splash! is:

- to affirm parents in their decision to have their child baptized.

We do this by:

- recognizing that right and wrong exist

- recognizing that we have choices about our lives

- encouraging some reflection about how to make positive choices

- introducing and explaining some baptism vocabulary and symbolism within that context.

Bubble-Talk – tuning in to God through prayer

Once people have had their child baptized, it's clearly A Good Thing to encourage the continuation of the relationship with God. But prayer has a numinous quality about it that can confuse people. How do you encounter and 'talk to' God? Bubble-Talk is about explaining how this encounter is different from meeting and talking to each other in our oh-so literal and material world.

This topic of prayer walks hand in hand with Storytime, because both prayer and Scripture are necessary elements of worship, but there is a particular reason why Storytime is placed last, which is explained below.

The main aim of Bubble-Talk is:

- to encourage parents to pray and for them in turn to encourage their children to pray.

We do this by:

- reflecting on the differences between human communication, verbal and non-verbal, and our interaction with God

- beginning to explain how to pray and what to expect

- broaching the idea that silence and stillness is part of prayer.

Storytime – opening the Scriptures

In the last session of the Starting Rite course, other family members are invited to take part. All the other sessions happen on a weekday morning; this one is held on a Saturday morning, so dads can come if they are willing and able.

The first time I ran a full-blown Starting Rite course, I used the last session, with an open invite to babies' friends and relations, to cover all four previous sessions. At this point in the Starting Rite development, there was no Bubble-Talk session; so we spent the fifth session doing a taster of Peek-a-

Boo!, How Much Love?, Splash! and Storytime. It didn't work partly because we tried to fit too much in; it felt rushed. The other reason was the difference in dynamics having dads around. One dad let me know that massaging his baby daughter in front of others felt uncomfortable and I could definitely appreciate this. It led me to consider the question 'what sort of religious topic or activity would dads feel most at ease with?' I discussed it with a friend from church and we decided stories were a safe bet. Dads, to varying degrees admittedly, would probably feel OK reading a story to their children.

Having said that, this is the one session where we don't sit and read a book together; there's more action, movement and practical hands-on tasks, which again may suit dads better. We enact three stories and, in doing so, we explain how to approach and interpret Bible stories. The point being that Starting Rite encourages carers to continue the practices learned on the course in the rest of their lives. In the case of Storytime, we aim to give them the tools to read and appreciate Scripture with their children in the comfort and privacy of their own home.

So the presence of dads at the fifth session is the main reason why Storytime is last, but there are a couple more. First, as this is the last session, it is wise to think about where are we pointing families to next? Our ministry for them does not stop at the end of a Starting Rite course. In our case, we encourage families to attend our mums and toddler service; and the focus of this service is a Bible story; so we often say 'we do more of this sort of thing in our pram service every Thursday, why not come along?' More generally, Storytime, with its emphasis on Scripture, does provide an appropriate bridge for other forms of children's ministry, such as Messy Church or Godly Play. Second, the very last activity of this session (and the whole course) is the story of the Exodus. Our understanding of Jesus Christ, of baptism and our salvation as a human race owes so much to this story that it feels very meet and right to culminate Starting Rite with the enactment of this epic narrative.

> ## In Storytime the main aim is:
>
> - to give parents the confidence to pick up Bible stories and read them to their children.
>
> Other aims are:
>
> - to draw attention to the many levels or layers associated with Bible stories
>
> - to give pointers on how to interpret or reflect on biblical narrative
>
> - to emphasize the great benefits of repeating the telling and retelling of these stories.

Hopefully this will have given you an idea of the outline of Starting Rite and the reasons for its shape and flow. While we're looking at the course as a whole, this is a good time to mention the place that the handouts, the carers' expectations and a photographic device (camera, phone, iPad, etc.) hold within Starting Rite.

Handouts

The role of handouts

We give handouts to the carers throughout the Starting Rite course. Before launching the Starting Rite course at my church, I talked to the mission enabler of our diocese, who suggested the idea of giving handouts. It would be, he advised, a way of sharing with other principal carers (dads in particular) what was covered in the session. This idea was truly inspired. The handouts also have the advantage of exploring in more depth the Christian beliefs covered in the session. This means the session itself can be baby-focused and allows carers the opportunity to give a voice to their thoughts. What the church has to say on these topics is on the handout; don't be tempted to try and explain it all in the group setting. Following some feedback from another church who have recently run the course, there is now an 'initial' handout that can be tailored to your church context; you can attach this to your first email contact with the carers. All the handouts are on the CD.

Taking contemporary culture into consideration

In the first chapter of this book, I talked about how Starting Rite values mission. We looked at how Church culture sometimes differs from contemporary culture and one area in which the Church can unfortunately do this is by telling or presenting the faith in a 'take it or leave it' kind of way. The handouts do present the Christian faith; but they try to provoke some reflection in the mind of the reader. One mum wrote on her feedback form: 'I would have liked a moment at the following session to discuss questions on the handout (not like homework!) as a group.' Another mum wrote: 'Maybe talk about own spiritual background/beliefs.' I was astonished to read these comments, but again they both demonstrate how current society prefers 'conversation' or shared exploration rather than lecture-style 'presentation'. They were seeking the opportunity for an open sharing and listening to others' reflections and ideas. The way I have dealt with this is to always offer an opportunity at the end of every session to talk about anything they want. Carers do come individually and discuss concerns they have; how to explain death to children for example. You may well think of other ways to listen and talk through the parents' own thoughts and beliefs.

Feedback about the handouts

Before the first Starting Rite course, I (of little faith) truly suspected that the handout would be lobbed in the nearest public bin as soon as the participant left the building. But not only have the feedback forms revealed that all the mums read nearly all the handouts, but I've also had comments such as:

'Kept them for reference.'
'Very informative and useful.'
'Good that they were laminated – allows you to keep them safe.'
'It would be nice to have some sort of folder to be able to keep the handouts in.'
'Clarified and summarized the day's session very well.'

'They backed up the sessions very well.'

Some mums have even quoted the handouts to me! It was also encouraging to see that the average number of handouts that dads read was three.

So despite my early scepticism, they have become an absolutely crucial part of the Starting Rite course. Sometimes I picture in my mind's eye a mum breastfeeding her baby in the peace and quiet of her home, reading one of the handouts about God's love: God can and does speak in the still small voice of calm. Please use them.

Carers' expectations

At the beginning of the course, we ask carers to write on post-its what their expectations of the course are. It is very useful to read what these are; generally speaking the main points that come through are:

- having fun or quality time with their baby
- bonding with their baby
- having a chance for them to meet other carers
- having a chance for their babies to meet other babies
- learning new things – songs, play activities for them to do with their baby
- giving exclusive time to their youngest child, rather than dividing attention between baby and other children.

But the expectations expressed that are most interesting for us are the ones about the faith aspect of the course and here it's probably most revealing when we listen to the carers' own voices:

'Introducing R [her baby] to religion.'
'Discuss religion in a relaxed atmosphere.'
'Explaining church and God in a childlike way for when they're older.'
'An opportunity to think about God and faith in a way which relates to me and my baby.'
'Understand a way of explaining God and in [this] respect death to my children in light of a recent bereavement.'
'Know how to introduce God to the life of Q [her baby].'
'How to introduce God to C [her baby].'

Not all participants are looking for any religious input; that is fine, as long as they know beforehand that Starting Rite is run by the church and is about faith. They may simply want the time to have fun and bond with their bundle of joy; they may become more interested as their child gets older.

At this point, it is useful to observe first that the expectations expressed so far fall within the remit of the two main aims of Starting Rite: 1) to give parents or carers an opportunity to focus on their baby; 2) to equip them for the nurture of their child's Christian faith.

The second observation is that the feedback forms reveal that all these expectations are met by the course. But before we sit complacently on our laurels, it is definitely worth consistently asking about expectations at the start of every course. This practice ensures that people do not come based on misunderstandings: for example, 'I thought I had to do the course to get my child christened'; 'I thought you would look after my baby so I could catch up on Facebook'; 'I thought you would gaze at a crystal, grant my son three wishes and predict a dazzlingly successful future for him', etc., etc. We certainly can't meet all expectations that may come up, but it's worth considering to what extent we can respond to different sorts of requests or comments. To do this, it's always best to measure the expectation against the main aims of Starting Rite and weigh up whether it can be accommodated.

Photos

It is useful to have photos to show your church and to offer as gifts to the families. However, this is not an essential part of the Starting Rite course. If you decide not to, you can skip this section.

If you are going to take photos, please read on. For safeguarding reasons, it is essential to ask the participants' permission to take photos of their child. You should explain exactly how the photos will be used – on public websites, on publicity (internal or external) material, and how securely and for how long they will be stored. Verbal permission may be sufficient, but you should check this with your church's safeguarding policy, your child protection coordinator or even your diocesan child protection officer.

The photos serve two purposes: 1) photos are part of your gift to the families at the end of the course; 2) you can use the pictures to present Starting Rite to the rest of your church at the Annual Parochial Church Meeting or at other times.

Giving photos to families

Throughout the course, at the more relaxed times of the sessions, take some portrait pictures of carer and baby or just the baby. Try to get action shots, where the baby is at play; these photos serve as a visual reminder of what we covered in the course. Print the photos out and distribute them to the families at the last session.

Taking it further

Why not be more creative? Design cards or frames with a baby picture and a Bible verse for the family. Make a baptism card with baby's face on and present to the family at the baptism service (see Chapter 11). Create a short booklet with a reminder of each session and put photos in where appropriate. Pre-school nurseries create lever arch folders of a child's learning journey full of photos, comments, observations and encouraging words about their progress. The possibilities are endless and only restricted by how much time you have on your hands.

Presenting Starting Rite to your church

It is extraordinarily difficult to articulate Starting Rite in words (think about how much text you have waded through in this book so far, and we haven't even started the course content yet). Remember Peter Privett: 'Play for children operates in the non-logical, non-verbal realms of language ... Adults prefer to operate in the logical world, the world of words and ideas.'[33]

Believe me it's a challenge to explain how a piece of netting and a shiny card illustrate the mystery of God *and* entertain a baby for one and a half hours. A slideshow of photos (or video) of tots wallowing in textiles, water, sand and bubbles does the job much better.

---

33 Anne Richards and Peter Privett (eds), *Through the Eyes of a Child*, London: Church House Publishing, 2009, p. 101.

The Song Book

On the CD that comes with this book, you will find the Song Book which contains a variety of songs and choruses that will be used in the course. All the songs in that book are either reproduced with permission or they are already in the public domain. You will however need to supplement this book with other songs that you feel will work within the session. The following chapters that explain how to run the sessions give suggestions of songs (marked 'suggestion' in brackets), but you will need to check the copyright permission before reproducing them in the Song Book. Your church should have a policy or guidelines about this. If your church has a CCLI licence, then use this website to check which Christian songs are covered: http://uk.search.ccli.com/

The list of songs that are not in the Song Book, but are suggested for use during the course are:

1,2,3, Jesus loves me
Jesus' love is very wonderful
We are marching in the light of God
Who made the twinkling stars?
With Jesus in the boat

If you are unsure of the tune of the songs, try looking them up on YouTube: https://www.youtube.com/

The next chapter will explain exactly how to lay out your equipment in your venue in preparation for your incoming group and general principles of leading the course.

5

Getting ready to welcome your families

You're standing in your clean, tidy, warm, carpeted (if necessary) space next to two boxes and a stack of baby changing mats. What happens next?

This chapter is about setting the scene in readiness to welcome your babies and their carers and explains why flexibility is key to running the sessions.

Setting up the room

It's not a bad idea to set up the night before your course actually starts, if this is possible. If you can't, just give yourself plenty of time, especially if you have to check health and safety or childproofing aspects of your venue every week. If your premises are used for other purposes, you may have to set up child-gates or block off radiators each time. So for a 9.30 am doors open, 10 am start, ensure you're there around 8 am.

Every week, you will need all the contents of the 'Set-Up box', listed in Chapter 3.

To give you a preview of how the group will be seated, have a look at this bird's eye view.

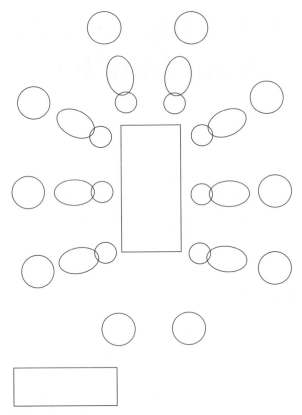

The leaders are the two circles at the bottom of the picture. The carers are seated in a horseshoe shape around the room; with babies (lying on changing mats) facing towards them. The rectangle in the middle is the central focal area, where a rug or blanket has been placed. The rectangle at the very bottom left of the picture is a table; this is to control babies' access to your resources; cameras generally need to be out of reach of babies for example; some of them will be mobile and can grab hold of and pull straps hanging down. The table can be placed anywhere behind you.

So start by laying out the **central blanket** in the middle of the room or carpet if you are using one. Place the **changing mats** in a horseshoe around the central blanket. The changing mats have raised edges on three sides and the side without a raised edge should be nearest the carer.

It does not matter whether the top end of the changing mats (and babies' heads) are on or off the rug.

If you have something for the carers to sit on – a **cushion** or **mat** – place these at the end of the changing mats, making a second concentric horseshoe around the room.

The leaders are allowed to sit on cushions too! Leaders can sit on chairs if sitting on the floor is problematic, but it would be best if the chair was as low as possible.

The **boxes of tissues, packets of wipes, kitchen roll** and **name cards** go onto the central blanket so participants can reach them.

The **Song Books** go next to every changing mat (not on them).

Have the **room thermometer** out on the table so you can get an accurate reading of the room temperature; it should be between 18° and 21°C.

Pin up your **door signs** on any external doors showing that the course is taking place and point people in the right direction towards your hall or venue.

Get your **leader's folder** and **list of participants** out ready.

All the other equipment – **biros, post-it notes, packets of antibacterial wipes, marker pens, camera** – can stay in the box on the table until they are needed.

This is your basic, bread-and-butter set-up for every week. Other sessions do require further preparation of the room, especially Splash!

Now have a cup of tea, pray about your participants and give it over to God.

Welcoming in

When the group begins to arrive, a continuous flow of welcome, friendliness, questions about baby, tea, coffee, biscuits and milk of human kindness is A Good Thing. Some mums may turn up at the first session having had four hours' sleep over the last seven nights; some may be terrified at coming to a group full of strangers; some may be suffering from post-natal depression. I have lone trekked and travelled in three different continents, but the prospect of going to a children's centre baby group for the first time scared me silly. Don't underestimate how hard it will be for some to make it through the door.

Name cards

As people are arriving, make sure that everyone has a name card that has either been filled in by you or by the participants. The name card should have the name of the baby and the carer; it's useful to distinguish which one is which; I underline the baby's name. The names on the cards should be easy to read by the leader and everyone else in the group.

Hot drinks: a health and safety warning

Our health visitors recently advised that hot drinks should be offered and consumed in one part of the premises and definitely not while holding a baby. Keep the hot drinks on a table or hatch or shelf well out of reach of children. Leave babies in car seats or on the mats with toys, while mum has her drink on the other side of the room. But it's still wise to remain alert. I once left a cuppa on the other side of a table from my two-year-old, who was in a highchair. I went out of the room, thinking 'no *way* can he reach that'. Thirty seconds later – screams from the kitchen. I ran in: he'd used the tablecloth to pull the mug across the table to get the drink and then tipped scalding tea all over him. Ergo: no tablecloths.

Towels

You will have asked your carers to bring a towel for their baby. When they have decided where to sit, they can place their towel on the changing mat in front of them, so baby is on something material and soft, rather than plastic. This doesn't really matter for most sessions, but the towel is important for Session 2, How Much Love?, and Session 3, Splash!

Babies and the need for flexibility

Happily for them, babies have no concept of time and timing. They may feel wide awake at 3 am or drop off just at the beginning of their christening service (and having your head dunked in cold water makes quite an awakening!). So flexibility is the name of the game with this course. This also fits in with the atmosphere you aim to create within the course; people should feel relaxed, comfortable, almost 'at home'.

Starting

If you advertise a 10 am start, don't be too anxious if no one's there at 9.55 am. Babies puke and poo just as you're ready to leave the house, so give carers a chance to change nappies, etc.

Often babies arrive asleep; talk to carers about whether they want to wait until baby wakes up or just allow them to be aroused from their slumbers by the lovely angelic singing!

It's always fine to wait a bit before starting; it allows carers to chat and you to get to know them and their babies.

During

The informal nature of the sessions means there is always time to 'chill'; activities can be extended or shortened or abandoned as and when and if babies respond. As the leader it's good to have an idea of the beginning and end, but be prepared to adapt the outline of the session according to what's going on. Carers' and babies' lives are dominated by three things:

Sleeping

One week, a little baby girl started crying, rising to screaming. Her mum looked at me and said, 'I won't pick her up; she just needs to go to sleep and she does this best by lying down.' We had started to sing some songs, so we just kept on singing songs (worked our way through most of the song Book). Whenever we stopped in between songs, she started crying again, but gradually calmed down and nodded off. Some carers strap the babies into the buggy and wheel them up and down in the room, while we're carrying on with the singing, bubble-blowing, splashing, etc.

Feeding

Some carers will need to feed their babies (breast or bottle) at some point in the hour and a half. Ensure you let them know this is perfectly OK; the course works around them.

Bottoms

For everyone's health and happiness, nappies need to be changed. This might mean carer and tot go out to the baby changing area; they are already on changing mats, so nappies can be changed in the group; whatever works for them. If there is a toddler in the room with mum (which sometimes happens) they will also need toilet access. One time, mum whipped out a potty; little one stripped down; potty was filled and then emptied into the neighbouring toilet without me noticing (someone told me it happened afterwards in case you're wondering). Give some thought about how to dispose of used nappies. Do you have a nappy bin or will you ask carers themselves to take them home? Most people are fine either way.

Ending

Your sessions aim to last an hour and a half. Sometimes they may be shorter; it's rarely been longer, because it's always good to have time to talk to people at the end. It's often at the end that carers come and tell us sometimes quite profound and personal stuff or ask advice about faith and their children. They also like to chat with each other while we're clearing up and that's fine too.

So now you're ready for starting let's turn our attention to what we actually do. In Part 2 we look at the sessions themselves.

Part 2

The Starting Rite
sessions

Session 1: Peek-a-Boo!

'I will make all my goodness pass before you ... But ... you cannot see my face; for no one shall see me and live.'

(Exodus 33.19–20)

Indeed, to this very day whenever Moses is read, a veil lies over their minds; when one turns to the Lord, the veil is removed. Now the Lord is the Spirit, and where the Spirit of the Lord is, there is freedom. And all of us, with unveiled faces, seeing the glory of the Lord as though reflected in a mirror, are being transformed into the same image from one degree of glory to another; for this comes from the Lord, the Spirit.

(2 Corinthians 3.15–18)

Why Peek-a-Boo!? A theological reflection

Have a read of these (genuine) quotes from children aged between three and five years old:

'Where is God?'
'Why can't we see God?'
'God is pretend because we can't see him.'
'Who made God?'
'What did God make us with?'
'When was God a baby?'
'Is God dead?'
'What would happen if we didn't have God in our world?'
'Can we see God when he's making things?'

'How can God be everywhere?'
'God is invisible.'[34]

If you were asked the first of those questions, 'Where is God?', how would you reply? To give an answer in normal, literal terms is seemingly impossible. We know God is with us all the time, but we can't see him all the time; the way we 'see' him is unlike how we 'see' material, or earthly, things.

It's helpful (and perhaps reassuring) to know that children are used to *not* understanding things fully:

> Children lack knowledge about many things. In every sentence there may be words they don't understand and many of the actions of those around them may be puzzling – why does Mummy disappear (to the kitchen)? *Mystery* is a close, mostly unthreatening, friend in childhood, and responding with *awe* or a *search for meaning* are everyday childhood games.[35]

God fills the world of childhood games so naturally. Trevor Dennis in many of his stories has God playing with his creation; in one story, God plays hide and seek with Adam and Eve.[36] This way of picturing the relationship between ourselves and God can also be used by the game of peek-a-boo.

A recent BBC news report talked about research taking place at Birkbeck College, in the University of London, into babies' sense of humour. The following is a quote from Dr Caspar Addyman, leading the research:

> Across all ages and all the countries we surveyed, peek-a-boo is by far and away the most favourite game. It's the absolute best combination of all the great things about laughter, so first of all there is a surprise there but it's a nice surprise, so mummy's gone away but 'oh thank goodness she's come back'. And second it's incredibly social; it's mummy, it's your favourite person in the world.[37]

---

34 With thanks to the reception children of Hall Orchard Primary School and their teacher, Miss L. Taylor, and the children from the Little Angels Pram Service, Holy Trinity Church, Barrow upon Soar.

35 Rebecca Nye, *Children's Spirituality*, London: Church House Publishing, 2009, p. 8.

36 Trevor Dennis, *Speaking of God*, London: SPCK, 1992, pp. 25–8.

37 Report by Claudia Hammond: www.bbc.co.uk/news/science-environment-24576803

The game peek-a-boo! lends itself very naturally as a play-metaphor for the mystery and revelation of God. It's one approach to understanding how we encounter God.

Aims for this session

The main aim of Peek-a-Boo! is:

- to evoke our awareness of God.

Other aims:

- to acknowledge that this awareness is difficult to articulate

- to promote the idea that mystery can be welcomed; that mystery can invite, not repel, trust in God

- to overthrow the taboo of talking about God.

What you need

For this session you will need your Peek-a-Boo! box (see Chapter 3), containing:

- Ten copies of *Peekaboo Baby!* by Mandy Ross
- Mirror cards
- Lots of different material (about 15–20 different pieces)
- Other peek-a-boo books, e.g. *Baby Faces Peekaboo!* (Dorling Kindersley), *Eyes, Nose, Toes, Peekaboo!* (Dorling Kindersley)
- Handouts. (All handouts are on the accompanying CD.)

Health and safety for Peek-a-Boo!

Peek-a-Boo! uses lots of different sorts of material. You may have found some in charity shops or odd remnants from home or fabric stores. It's important to make sure that the frayed edge of the piece is hemmed or sewn up to stop loose threads falling away. Remove or sew tightly buttons, sequins, tassels or other loose decorations. Babies could swallow or end up entangled in threads, etc., so they're best avoided.

How to run the Peek-a-Boo! session

Once you've read all the chapters on the five sessions, and feel familiar with the content of the course, you might find you can use the session overviews to help you run the sessions. The overviews act as a sort of 'service sheet' or running order.

Please note in all sessions there is a LOT of singing. You'll be amazed though at how readily participants join in, because they see how much joy it gives their offspring; sometimes the babies even babble an accompaniment! The first time I went to a baby group there were about twenty carers with babies and it was quite astonishing to hear the chorus of voices that boomed out 'Twinkle, twinkle, little star'!

Session overview

Song:[38]   'Hello everyone, how are you?' *(all the songs are in alphabetical order in the Song Book)*

Introductions

Songs: 'Clap your hands'
             '1,2,3, Jesus loves me' *(suggestion)*

Post-its – write down any EXPECTATIONS for these sessions.
Material; different sorts – choose two or three.

---

38 Song Books are available on the accompanying CD.

Song: 'Can you play at peek-a-boo?'

Children are comfortable with this game; the way we 'see' and not 'see'/sense God is quite similar.

Songs: 'Where is …? Where is …?' *(Frere Jacques)*
              'Open, shut them'

Some people have a sudden or unexpected feeling that they've sensed something beyond themselves. Maybe on top of a mountain, maybe watching a sunset, maybe in a holy place.

Read: *Peekaboo Baby!* books

Q: How did you choose the name for your baby?

Mirror cards

Made in the image of God: we reflect God. God works through us; we communicate his love and goodness to the world and to our children. What they learn of God is through you.

Peekaboo books, mirror cards, material – open play.

Songs: 'My God is so big'
              'The little green frog'

Baby record book

Prayer with children; post-its. Anything to give thanks for about your baby; anything that concerns you.

Song: 'He's got the whole world in his hands'

Handouts!

Next week: massage. Oil preferences. Bring towel!

Blessing

Detailed description of the Peek-a-Boo! session

As I said in the previous chapter, flexibility is the name of the game. Please don't surge on regardless of what is happening among the little ones. Change and adapt as necessary. Recently a group from a nearby church came to visit our Starting Rite course with the intention of running one themselves. They attended two sessions, two of them at a time. After both sessions, they all noted how much more relaxed the sessions were than they had expected. They had read the session guidelines below, but observed to me at the end of the session that there was a lot more 'chill-out' time than they had anticipated. They pointed out the importance of allowing time for the parents to discuss teething, weaning and other issues among themselves. Although what follows seems highly structured and prescriptive, the atmosphere and running of the sessions should be extremely relaxed and informal.

Songs and introductions

At some point in the first fifteen minutes, introduce yourself, your helpers, and say something about what the course offers. You could mention how it's a chance to meet other carers; it will suggest ideas of what to do with their baby – songs, activities and so on, but it is specifically to help them think about the spiritual nurture of their child.

When you manage to say those things will depend on whether some of the babies are fussing right at the start; if they are, then try singing ASAP. Singing has a magically soothing effect on babies and can calm them down as if you were a fairy godmother waving a wand. When babies are a bit calmer, jump in there with your introductions about yourselves and the course.

We generally always start with the same three songs: 'Hello everyone, how are you?', 'Clap your hands', and '1,2,3, Jesus loves me'. You are welcome to use any songs you prefer that suit the beginning of a session. Music and words are all good value stuff for babies' development, but do add in actions and exaggerated gesture where appropriate.

The song 'Hello everyone, how are you?' works well because you go round the group saying the name of the babies, looking at them and waving, for example:

'Hello Luke, how are you?
Hello Natasha, how are you?

Hello Dylan, how are you?'
and so on ...

This way, everyone learns the babies' names quite well! It's also a way of socializing babies; you are introducing them to the idea of greeting people when you see them for the first time that day. Gestures for this song could include waving for 'hello' and the thumbs-up sign when you're singing 'I'm very well, thank you.'

The song 'Clap your hands' is good bonding material for mums and babies. Clapping can be a bit loud, so moderate accordingly. Just before verse 3, you could pause to give carers time to pick up their baby. Then, holding baby firmly but not tightly under their armpits, either facing carer or the group, move him/her up (dads tend to throw them!) and down several times.

Note: If you have a very small baby (under two months), you can't be wobbling them around as their wee brains get knocked about in ways that nobody's thrilled about; advise mum to gently rock her little one. Most carers have a sense of what is appropriate movement.

You can sing different verses faster or more slowly as you feel led.

'1,2,3, Jesus loves me' is one for babies to watch. Use gestures to point to 'me', 'you' and count with fingers.

Post-its – Expectations for the course

Now hand out some post-its and a pen to each adult participant. Ask them to write down their expectations of the course. Explain that you will read their expectations and if there are some that would not normally be met, we'll try to accommodate them if possible.

This is one of the best times to go round and greet babies and play with them while their carer is scribbling away. If your church has a children's corner or crèche cupboard, grab some age-appropriate toys to offer babies who are getting restless while mum's attention is elsewhere. You can also start to put out the pieces of material; just drop them in the centre of the room on the blanket or rug. Gather up the post-its and put them away in a box on the table (if you leave them out, babies simply eat them – no kidding).

Material and songs

Invite the carers to grab a couple of pieces of material. The babies may already have started to show an interest in a piece, that's all fine and dandy. Explain that we'll be singing some songs while playing peek-a-boo. Get them to start playing the game. Some babies might want to hold the material themselves; some carers might 'hide' and this may upset their tot; if so, stop and just let him watch others or allow baby to mess around in the material. Hopefully you will have different sorts of textures – a four-month-old may never have felt netting before and I mean *never, ever, ever*; it may be terrifying or exciting or just weird; who knows what's going on? But give them time to get used to it!

After a bit, start singing some peek-a-boo songs. There are a few in the Song Book, but if you know and prefer others, use them.

Comment

When you've done a couple of these songs, you might throw out a comment about how children talk about God, and they often have questions about him. I generally say something along the lines of the following:

> Children enjoy playing this game; the way we 'see' and not 'see' or sense God is quite similar to this game.
>
> Some people have a sudden or unexpected feeling that they've sensed something beyond themselves. Maybe on top of a mountain, maybe watching a sunset, maybe in a holy place, like a cathedral. That sense is a sense of God.

Make sure you're responding to the reaction of the babies. You might want to sing a bit more in between your comments. If anyone wants to respond to what you've said, that's fine. The important thing about the comments is that they are short. These sessions are baby-focused. The more you talk to the adult participants, the less attention you give to babies. The little you do say may need quite a lot of time to reflect on.

Coffee break

This might be a good time for another cuppa or, if everything is going well, wait until after the book reading.

Book

Give out the *Peekaboo Baby!* books. Ensure the babies are able to look at the book. Some may not be interested in the book at this point; that's OK. If none are, then have a break or sing a song. Then try again. You can abandon the book altogether, but we've never had to do this. Get everyone to read together and allow time for flap opening and closing!

If you haven't had a break, it's probably a good moment to do so.

Question for carers

After a while, when babies have been changed or fed or whatever is necessary, ask the carers why they chose that name for their child. It's absolutely fascinating to hear the reasons; sometimes there are some very deep and moving replies.

If a child has been adopted or is being fostered, this may be more difficult to establish; although carers might have found out the meaning of the name. Parents of adopted children might be thinking of giving their child an additional name; you could mention that names can be legally added to a child at baptism.

Mirror cards

Hand out the mirror cards; it's good to give one silver mirror card and one of a different colour. Ask carers to show their baby the card and the reflection of themselves in it. Allow the babies to hold the card if they can. Allow them time to play with them. They generally lick, chew, butt them and spread saliva and/or snot over them. Again this is all fine; it's simply about exploring and experiencing. Carers can show a reflection of their image to their child. Allow for a time of open play at this point with material, mirror cards and books. This could include a comment.

Comment

I often say something like:

> You may have heard that we are made in the image of God: we reflect God. God works through us; we communicate his love and goodness to the world and to our children. What they learn of God is through you. The mirror cards illustrate how we reflect God.

Relax, chat, take photos

A lot of the course is about relaxing and chatting with carers and babies. These are the times when you start to get to know them and they you. I can't think of many nicer ways of spending a morning than making a baby giggle and then sitting down with a cup of tea. Make the most of it! You can also use this time to take a few photos. Remember to tell everyone what you'll be using the photos for (see Chapter 4, section on photos).

Songs

About twenty minutes before the end of the session, or sooner if everyone's getting restless, start singing a few songs. It doesn't matter which ones, just choose ones you or the participants like.

Baby record book and post-its

Give out the post-its again and ask the carers to write down one or two things they absolutely love about their baby. The usual suspects are things like 'her cornflower blue eyes'; 'his guttural giggle'; 'the dimple in his left elbow'; 'the curl at the nape of her neck'; stuff like that. Ask them also to write down anything they are worried about or struggling with: 'waking up fifteen times a night'; 'cradle cap'; 'teething', for example. Explain a bit about prayer and how they can turn those little notes into prayers. Things we delight in about our children are a cause for thanksgiving; sometimes people want their child baptized as a way of giving thanks for such a miracle. Worries or concerns are intercessions. It's fine to say 'Dear God, I'm worried about George's teeth. He's really miserable. Amen.' Be reassuring about how simple it is to pray.

The point about the baby record book is to encourage the carers to add information to it. They can stick the post-its into the record book for future reference. If they feel it's inappropriate for their child to see the comments later on in life, they can remove them. The book also acts as a surrogate prayer diary. If the carers do pray, and see their prayers answered, this can be very powerful.

Song

We generally finish with the same song: 'He's got the whole world in his hands'. We also go round the room naming the children, 'He's got Luke and Natasha in his hands, he's got Dylan and Benjamin in his hands', and so on. This reminds you again of their names!

Handouts!

It is very easy (as I have found so often to my cost) to forget the handouts. Make sure you distribute these before everyone leaves! The handouts as we've noted earlier elaborate on the topic of the session.

Notices about the following week

Tell everyone that next week we will be doing the session called How Much Love?. The session involves baby touch with oil. Ask carers if they know whether their babies are allergic to any particular oil. Tell them you normally use Johnson's baby oil but can also bring vegetable oil. If their baby is sensitive to either of these, ask them to bring their own oil. Essential oils are *not* appropriate for baby massage. See the health and safety advice in the next chapter. Remind them to bring a towel because their baby will be stripped down and may feel chilly on a changing mat.

Blessing

Choose a suitable blessing or a short prayer – for example, the grace – to finish.

As everyone's packing up, help them collect their gear or hold their baby for them while they do so. Some may want to talk to you about something church related, which is great; allow time for this.

Et voilà! Now all you have to do is clear up!

Wipe down the changing mats with an antibacterial wipe. Keep the setting-up box stuff separate from the session-specific items. You will need some of the material again for Storytime, so that could be moved to the Storytime boxes. Otherwise the mirror cards and the books will not be needed until your next course.

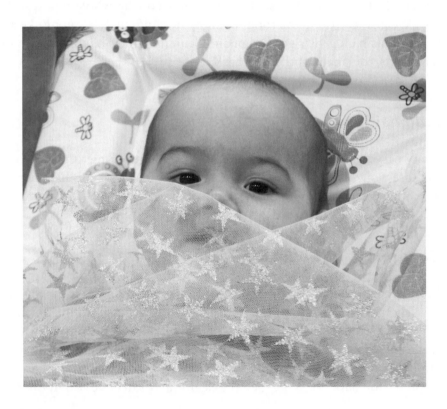

Session 2: How Much Love?

And the man and his wife were both naked, and were not ashamed.

(Genesis 2.25)

I led them with cords of human kindness, with bands of love. I was to them like those who lift infants to their cheeks. I bent down to them and fed them.

(Hosea 11.4)

I pray that you ... may have the power to comprehend, with all the saints, what is the breadth and length and height and depth, and to know the love of Christ that surpasses knowledge, so that you may be filled with all the fullness of God.

(Ephesians 3.18–19)

Why How Much Love? A theological reflection

God loves his creation perfectly. As Christians we are called to reflect that love both towards him and his world. The vast majority of parents try to demonstrate a similar sort of love towards their children. This love shown to children from the very beginning of life, when they are at their most vulnerable, leads them to trust: 'the naked child only has the confidence to go out and encounter the world, to play in it, to have fun in it and to risk the danger of it, if the child knows that the adults in his/her life stand behind to protect and to help in case of difficulty'.[39] For healthy and loving relationships to

39 Anne Richards and Peter Privett (eds), *Through the Eyes of a Child*, London: Church House Publishing, 2009, p. 35.

exist, there has to be trust, not only between humans but also between us and God. As Rebecca Nye says:

> Spirituality involves trusting. In the first instance, trust is needed because spirituality does not usually deal in empirical evidence, visions or voices. Trust is comfortable with different kinds of knowing, and not knowing, evidenced by a strong tradition in spiritual literature.
>
> Trust is also essential to the maintenance of spiritual life – trusting that there's still value when this life feels all dried up, baffling or more than we can take. This kind of trust encourages us not to run away or raise our barriers.[40]

Like any baby or child with their principal carer, we are only likely to trust in God – to put our most vulnerable selves before God – if we feel sure that we will be met with loving understanding, wisdom, safety and protection. With God, the more we trust in or enter into God's love, the more we understand it and the more we trust in it. In time, we become aware that this love is wholly trustworthy because it is utterly boundless and immeasurable. The reason why the book *Guess How Much I Love You* is used in this session is because it offers a wonderfully accurate picture of that love.

The book echoes the psalmist's words in Psalm 139.7–12:

> Where can I go from your spirit?
> Or where can I flee from your presence?
> If I ascend to the heaven, you are there;
> if I make my bed in Sheol, you are there.
> If I take the wings of the morning
> and settle at the farthest limits of the sea,
> even there your hand shall lead me,
> and your right hand shall hold me fast.
> If I say, 'Surely the darkness shall cover me,
> and the light around me become night,'
> even the darkness is not dark to you;
> the night is as bright as the day,
> for darkness is as light to you.

---

40 Rebecca Nye, *Children's Spirituality*, London: Church House Publishing, 2009, p. 54.

Bringing babies back to their naked selves, where they expect/await/hope for a loving touch that assures them of their parents' deep affection and longing for their flourishing, mirrors the opening scenes of Genesis where Adam and Eve, naked, free and unashamed, shared life fully and closely with God. Anne Richards draws a connection between nakedness and closeness to God through the act of massage:

> It is interesting that in our own society obsessed with fashion and clothes, people often turn to spiritual, healing experiences, or practices to promote well-being, which require the removal of clothes and the experience of touch. Many people enjoy saunas, massage, immersion in water at blood heat and other therapies which involve their skin being touched. Perhaps this is precisely because we want (or have missed) the child's experience of being naked in the environment and experiencing touch sensations which add to a sense of being close to God.[41]

Aims for this session

The main aim of How Much Love? is:

- to invite people into a knowledge of God's unboundaried love for us.

We do this by:

- establishing that God's nature is loving

- reassuring that we can trust God, because of his love for us

- wondering about the extent of God's love.

---

41 Richards and Privett (eds), *Through the Eyes*, p. 37.

What you need

For this session you will need your How Much Love? box, containing:

- 9 copies of *Guess How Much I Love You* board book by Sam McBratney
- 1 copy of *Guess How Much I Love You* soft cloth book
- 1 copy of *I Love You* by Giles Andreae
- 5 Baby Massage posters
- 9 small plastic travel bottles
- 1 large bottle of baby oil
- Funnels
- Handouts.

Extra setting up

Alongside the normal set-up, for this session you need to provide a bottle of oil for each participant. Use the funnel to help you pour out the oil into the smaller bottles. The kitchen paper in the 'Set-Up box' is useful for mopping up spillage.

Be aware that the posters curl up a lot. It's worth laying them out flat with weights in each corner well before the session starts.

Health and safety for How Much Love?

Oil

The main concern for this session is the oil that is used. I have always used either Johnson's baby oil or a vegetable oil, such as rapeseed. Essential oils must be avoided. The International Association of Infant Massage (IAIM) website recommends 'an unscented vegetable oil, preferably organically grown and cold pressed if possible'. It does not recommend olive oil. It is worth having a look at their website.[42] Do ask carers to think about skin allergies. If they have any concern at all, they should contact their health visitor or GP to check whether it is OK for them to use oil on their child.

42 www.iaim.org.uk/index.htm

Leading baby touch

It's good to remember that we are not aiming to teach carers how to massage their baby. We are using it as a springboard for reflection about a child's spiritual health and development. It's probably wise to use the term 'baby touch', rather than 'baby massage', otherwise carers might think you are a qualified baby massage instructor. If you want to train and be certified in baby massage, go to the IAIM website (see note 42 on p. 106) to read more.

You might be able to find someone who is trained and would voluntarily lead the massage aspects of the session for you. You could also approach a local children's centre to find out if they run baby massage courses for parents; if they do, ask about whether they would help you to learn more about it. Some centres provide booklets for parents; they may allow you to take some of these away with you.

If you are not trained, read and inwardly digest the baby massage poster carefully. At the beginning of the session tell the participants that you are leading them through the instructions on the poster, rather than teaching them how to massage. Another good source of information about baby massage is on the Johnson's Baby website: www.johnsonsbaby.co.uk/baby-massage/how-to-massage#baby-massage-guides. There are three guides: newborn; 2 to 6 months and 6 months+; it's worth reading them all. Note that you can massage very young babies – under two months – but it might be better to keep baby's clothes on (sometimes known as dry massage) and concentrate on legs, feet, tummy and back.

Room temperature

Make sure the temperature is appropriate for babies in their birthday suits; 18–21°C is about right.

How to run the How Much Love? session

Session overview

Songs: 'Hello everyone, how are you?'
              'Clap your hands'
              '1,2,3 Jesus loves me' (*suggestion*)

Last week – any thoughts?

Baby touch – give out oil and posters.
   We are working through the instructions on the poster.
   Be gentle and keep oiling hands.
But before starting, sing:

Song: 'Heads, shoulders, knees and toes'

  Strip baby down.
  Put oil on hands.
  Let's read the instructions at the top of the poster.

  Tummy and chest.

Song: 'What shall we do with a bouncing baby?'

Some churches use oil in baptism when they sign the baby with a cross. Give more information about the oil if your church uses it.

  Arms and hands.

Songs: 'Tommy thumb'
              'One finger, one thumb'

Q: What do you like about being a parent/carer?

  Legs and feet.

Songs: 'This little piggy'
              Verse 2 of 'One finger, one thumb'

Q: How would you describe your feelings towards your baby/children?

Face.

Song: 'From my head down to my toes'

Q: How would you describe their feelings towards you?
   Carry on baby touch or dress babies.

Read: *Guess How Much I Love You* books.

How you love your baby is similar to the way God loves us.

Song: 'Jesus' love is very wonderful' (*suggestion*)

Baby record book.

Prayer with children; post-its. You might like to write down some of the feelings you talked about; stick them in the book.

Song: 'He's got the whole world in his hands'

Handouts!

Next week: baby bathing. Towel!

Blessing

Detailed description of the How Much Love? session

Invite carers to lay their towel down on the changing mat underneath baby.

Songs and introductions

Once everyone has gathered and settled; start with the regular songs. As I said before, you can choose any. 'Hello everyone, how are you?', 'Clap your hands' and '1,2,3, Jesus loves me' work for us, so we use them every week.

Mention last week's session; briefly recap what was touched on; ask if anyone wants to say anything or ask any questions. (In my experience, they never do at this point; but they sometimes do at the end of the session.) Remind everyone that you're available to talk at any point during or after the session.

Introduce this week's session, How Much Love? I normally explain this as exploring God's love for us and we'll talk a bit about this while doing some baby touch.

Baby touch

Give out the bottles of oil to each carer and lay down the posters so that everyone has sight of one. Key points to make:

Be gentle

The touch of the strokes you are making should be gentle. Do not apply more pressure to the baby's limbs than you would normally while holding them. It is not like adult massage.

Top up with oil

While doing the strokes, it is important to keep your hands well-oiled. The baby's skin should not be dragged or tugged; so make sure you keep topping up with oil from the bottle. There is plenty of oil!

Song

'Heads, shoulders, knees and toes' is an appropriate song because it's a way of evoking in the babies an awareness of their bodies and also preparing them for the baby touch. You can sing it a few times; sometimes faster, sometimes slower.

Baby touch

Ask the carers to strip the babies down to their nappies. Keep nappies on, because otherwise you're looking at wee puddles all around. If they want to massage baby's bum, they can do it at home.

You might want to use a large doll to illustrate the actions outlined in the poster.

Start reading aloud the instructions at the top of the poster while asking carers to pour some oil onto their hands.

Get them started on the strokes for the tummy and chest. Once they are following the instructions well and repeating the actions, you could sing 'What shall we do with a bouncing baby?' (tune of 'What shall we do with the drunken sailor?'). Improvise the words according to the stroke you're doing; 'we'll stroke, stroke, stroke their chest/tummy', for example.

Be flexible – although the plan is to follow the poster's guidance on which area of the body to work on, there is no need to stick rigidly to this.

Some babies might strongly object to being massaged. Some might enjoy it for ten minutes and then feel they've had enough. Fine; mum can just join in the songs.

Some parents work at different paces to others. There'll be those who move very quickly through the strokes and cover the whole body, while others are still repeating the chest movements. It doesn't really matter. Those who have finished can start again or return to the limb that connects with the song you're about to launch into next.

Comment

At this point, I talk about the oil that some churches use in the baptism service. It's up to you how much of the following you would want to talk about. My spiel runs something like this:

> Most people don't notice it; but oil is used to make the sign of the cross on the baptism candidate's forehead. This oil is not any old oil from Tesco's Value range. The day before Good Friday – Maundy Thursday – there is a special service that takes place every year in all Anglican cathedrals. At this service three huge jugs of oil are blessed by the bishop. Traditionally each church from across the diocese brings three little phials or pots or containers and has them filled with these special oils. The three oils have

different uses; one of which is for baptism. Throughout our faith history oil has played an important role; it carries a sense of honouring, of anointing, of commissioning. Every British monarch, even today, is anointed with oil at their coronation. Oil is like God's love for us; when you apply oil, it rubs in to us and becomes part of us.

Baby touch and songs

Carry on following the instructions for massaging baby's arms and hands. Sing 'Tommy Thumb' and do the actions. Carers can stroke the appropriate finger for each line of the song if they want. You can sing other songs – 'One finger, one thumb', for example.

Question for carers

Ask participants what they like about being a carer (if you know all the participants are mums, then you can use the word 'mum'). Take mental note of what is said. This question often overlaps with the next one: how would they describe their feelings towards their baby? Again try to remember what is talked about. Unlike in Peek-a-Boo!, the questions here are beginning to be quite personal, so tread softly and kindly.

Baby touch and songs

Carry on following the instructions for massaging baby's legs and feet. Sing 'This little piggy' and do the actions. Carers can wiggle the appropriate toe for each line of the song if they want. Sing verse 2 of 'One finger, one thumb' – i.e. 'One leg, one foot, keep moving'.

Question for carers

If you feel the second question has not already been covered, then ask it now: how would they describe their feelings towards their baby? Again try to remember what is talked about.

Baby touch and songs

Carry on following the instructions for massaging baby's face. Sing 'From my head down to my toes' and do the actions, touching the right part of the face as appropriate.

Question for carers

You could ask (but I don't always, depending on time) how carers think their children feel towards them. Give time for reflection on this one.

Coffee break

Most babies will probably be ready to get dressed by this point. And everyone else will probably be ready for a cup of something. Have a break and relax. Put out any other books that you may have brought along, for example, *I Love You* by Giles Andreae. Take photos.

Book

Give out the *Guess How Much I Love You* books. As in the previous session, ensure the babies are able to look at the book and get everyone to read together. This book is quite long for babies to concentrate on, so keep the pace moving or even skip over a page or two. If you have a tiny baby (under two months), give them the soft cloth book; they can grip it and feel the velvety texture of the book.

This book illustrates the relationship between God and his people very powerfully. Remain flexible, but try to ensure this story is read at some point in the session.

Comment

You can start by noting that 'the way you love your baby is similar to the way God loves us'.

Repeat some of the feelings the carers expressed earlier. Pick up on those that would appropriately describe God's love for us. For example, 'I want the best for my baby'; 'God wants the best for us;' 'I just love being with her'; 'God loves being with us, sharing in our joys and sorrows'. Comments like 'I would feel angry if someone hurt them' need more careful handling.

Song

The words of the song 'Jesus' love is very wonderful' continue the theme and message of the book that's just been read.

Baby record book and post-its

Suggest to the parents that they might like to write down some of the feelings they talked about on the post-its and then stick them in the book. Again these thoughts can be turned into prayers: 'God, I feel so protective about Charlie; I pray for strength to protect him from harm as best I can', for example.

Song

Finish with the closing song: 'He's got the whole world in his hands', as for last week.

Handouts!

Don't forget handouts.

Notices about the following week

Tell everyone that next week we'll be using a baby bath, so they need to bring a towel again. Spares will be available, but it's best if they try to remember their own.

Blessing

Choose a suitable blessing or a short prayer – the grace, for example – to finish.

By now, you'll have got into the rhythm of the sessions. So chat to carers as they leave, clearing and gearing up for next week. Wipe down the changing mats with an antibacterial wipe.

Nothing from the How Much Love? box is needed in other sessions, so that box can be put back into storage. The small travel bottles get very oily on the outside; not nice for the next course! So I always clean them after this session (a painstaking job, as they can't go in the dishwasher!).

Note: Splash! needs a lot of setting up, so make sure you're ready to arrive early next time.

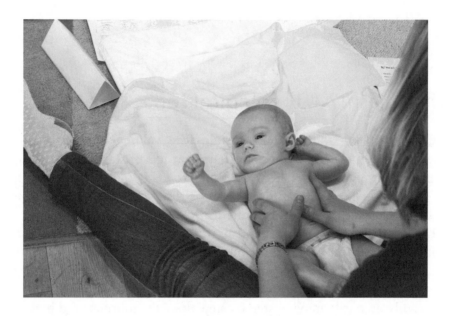

Session 3: Splash!

Choose life so you and your descendants may live, loving the Lord your God, obeying him and holding fast to him;

(Deuteronomy 30.19–20)

Proclaiming a baptism of repentance for the forgiveness of sins.

(Luke 3.3)

Why Splash!? A theological reflection

In Chapter 1 we talked about Starting Rite valuing mission. You may remember the Engel scale, the continuum that marks stages along the gradual process of becoming a Christian, 0 or zero being the point of repentance and conversion (see Chapter 1, p. 26). It is recognized that people come to faith sometimes suddenly and dramatically, but often slowly perhaps even cautiously. When it comes to baptism, the Church can have a tendency to stand at that 0 point or 'finishing line' of conversion, peremptorily tapping its foot hurrying people to 'cross the line', 'get there', believe all the right things and mean them. But how much does the Church support those who are steadily or warily moving step by step along the journey, and how much does it put itself in their shoes as they do so?

Splash! is the session that explicitly addresses baptism. But it does this by evoking the ideas and beliefs of this Christian rite from a different angle. We start from the assumption that parents want their children to grow up healthy in mind and body and to flourish in life. What happens if we start to look at this more closely? Questions arise: What is good and healthy for children? The two key elements of baptism, light and water, are universally recognized as good for humanity (indeed for all creation), and these are incorporated in experiential ways in the Splash! session. But how about exploring more probing questions: What is good for children to play with? To learn? To be influenced by? What is good for children to value? What are good choices for children to make as they grow up?

As baptism is a public declaration of choices or decisions that we have made: 'I turn to Christ'; 'I repent of my sins'; 'I renounce evil', it seems appropriate to ask what is the best choice and what would be the worst choice that we could make in life? And that is what we do in the Splash! session. Of course, when we ask these questions to committed Christian parents, the answer is something like, 'the best choice for my child would be for him/her to follow Christ' which mirrors the answer in the baptism service: 'I turn to Christ.' When we put this question to the carers who come on the course, most of the answers revolve around avoiding drugs and excessive alcohol consumption, resisting unhealthy peer pressure, keeping close to family and friends and adopting their values. Presumably, the reason why Christian parents don't say all these things is because they probably feel that following Christ would encompass all that will work for their child's good, wholesome development and flourishing. We have all that we need in Christ: 'God is able to make all grace abound to you, so that in all things at all times, having all that you need, you will abound in every good work' (2 Corinthians 9.8).

As we noted in Chapter 1, Starting Rite does not necessarily lead people to the point of conversion; it simply starts or maybe rekindles a process of reflection. It tries to accompany them as they think through their own values and beliefs and as they ponder how the Christian faith reflects those values and how it can have meaning and influence in their lives and the lives of their children. It is worth noting that at the moment of their child's baptism, even if they have not arrived at a point where we may feel they 'should be'– slain in the Spirit, praying in tongues, tithing their income and taking full responsibility for washing the church linen – they have started to turn and move in the right direction.

Aims for this session

The main aim of Splash! is:

- to affirm those parents who have decided to have their child baptized.

We do this by:

- recognizing that right and wrong exist

- recognizing that we have choices about our lives

- encouraging some reflection about how to make positive choices

- introducing and explaining some baptism vocabulary and symbolism within that context.

What you need

For this session you will need your Splash! box, containing:

- 10 copies of *God Knows All About Me* by Claire Page
- NSPCC *Art for Baby* book
- Tarpaulin
- Bath thermometer
- Towels
- Sponges
- Electric tealights
- Plastic scallop-shaped shell
- Handouts
- *Blackout tent/sensory den*
- *Cement mixer trays*

The last two items will not fit into the box, but are also part of this session.

Extra setting up

Splash! requires a lot of setting up. Give yourself plenty of time.

Tent or sensory den

In one corner of the room, but outside the normal 'horseshoe' area of changing mats, you need to set up the blackout tent or den. This may need more than one person to put together. You could, if you have the facilities, put the tent in another room, especially if this room is dark. If the tent has just a ground-sheet, then it might be good to cover the area with a blanket or cushions. Inside the tent, place some electric tealights. At this point they can be switched off.

Cement mixer trays

In another corner, but also away from the changing mats, cover the floor with the tarpaulin sheet. Place the mixer trays on top; the sponges, the plastic shell and the bath thermometer in the trays. Have some spare towels handy. Don't put water in yet, but make sure you can fill a bucket or jugs with some warm water fairly easily.

Health and safety for Splash!

Water

Parental vigilance: As there is a risk involved with water, remind parents or carers to be next to their child at all times while the baby is in the water. It is their responsibility to ensure the child's safety in and around water.

Temperature: When you fill the mixer trays, make sure the water is warm, not hot. The baby bath thermometer should indicate a comfortable temperature, but you can also ask the carers to check it themselves.

Depth of water: You can simply cover the base of the shallower mixer tray with water; say, 2–5 cm deep. The other tray can hold a greater water depth (10–15 cm). It's good and more amusing if there's plenty of splashing material.

Tealights

Babies do put tealights in their mouth. Make sure therefore that the lights are shatterproof. Better still, try to find some plastic containers to put the tealights in. I found some mug-height, frosted-plastic, tube-shaped tealight holders.[43] The babies grind their gums on the holder, with the flickering tealight inside.

How to run the Splash! session

Session overview

Songs: 'Hello everyone, how are you?'
           'Clap your hands'
           '1,2,3, Jesus loves me' (suggestion)

Recap of last 2 sessions.

Q1: What would be the worst choice your child could make in life?
Q2: What would be the best choice your child could make in life?

Divide into two groups

Blackout tent with tealights (one leader with this group)

Songs in the tent: 'Twinkle, twinkle'
                     'I see the moon'
                     'Who made the twinkling stars' (suggestion)

Any answers – Q1?

---

43 The ones I use are no longer produced. The tealights and holders I recommend in Chapter 3 under Equipment does not specify the material the holders are made of. It would be good to check this.

Baby bath (other leader with this group)

Songs in the bath: 'Row, row, row your boat'
                         '5 little ducks went swimming one day'

Any answers – Q1?

Swap over groups and answers to Q2.

Regroup

Read: *God Knows All About Me* books

Talking about choices and sitting in darkness and light. This symbolizes the Christian beliefs about Jesus being the light of the world.
    'Jesus spoke to them, saying, "I am the light of the world. Whoever follows me will never walk in darkness but will have the light of life"' (John 8.12). Baptism liturgy: 'God calls us out of darkness into his marvellous light' ... 'May almighty God deliver you from the powers of darkness ... and lead you in the light and obedience of Christ.'

Songs: 'We are marching in the light of God' (*suggestion*)
              'The Spirit lives to set us free'

Baby record book

Prayer with children; post-its. Write down the best choices your child could make in life

Song: 'He's got the whole world in his hands'

Handouts!

Next week: Bubble-Talk about prayer. Numbers for Saturday morning.

Blessing

Detailed description of the Splash! session

After tea and coffee has been consumed, gather carers around, settle babies on the changing mats or laps.

Songs and introductions

As I said before, you can choose any introductory songs, but we stick regularly to 'Hello everyone, how are you?', 'Clap your hands' and '1,2,3, Jesus loves me'.

Again talk briefly about the last two weeks' sessions and ask if anyone wants to say anything, offer a comment about the handouts or put forward any questions. Remind everyone that you're available to talk at any point during or after the session.

Introduce this week's session: Splash! Something along these lines works for me:

> Splash! looks at some of the symbols in baptism: the use of water and light, so we'll be splashing about in the water trays and sitting in a blackout tent! There's also some questions for you to think about.

Questions for carers

Give the questions now, because they require some thinking about.

> Q1: What would be the worst choice your child could make in life?
> Q2: What would be the best choice your child could make in life?

You're not expecting answers right now.

Divide into two groups

Halve the group. You take group one into the tent; group two will go with the other leader to the baby bath. Both leaders should talk through Q1 – 'worst choice' – while in the bath or den.

At this point, warm water needs to be poured into the trays. Ask carers to check the temperature. If you are taking group two, skip to the heading 'Baby bath' on p. 124.

Tent/den

Get everyone to squash up into the tent. Make sure the babies are comfortable (and the carers for that matter!). Switch on all the tealights (the carers can help with this). Show the tealights to the babes. If you can and it feels right, make the tent or den as dark as possible, so that the tealights really stand out. The atmosphere tends to generate a stillness and quietness among the babies but if you have one that violently objects, let them out quick!

Songs in the tent/den

You can sing any songs to do with light or darkness. The ones we use are: 'Twinkle, twinkle' and 'I see the moon' (not exactly a song, more of a rhyme).

Question for carers

This particular part of the course is for me one of the most poignant. Some of the answers are very moving. Remember that this course is not a parenting course; it's not about teaching how to raise children. The idea is always to get people thinking about their child's spiritual nurture. It is a beginning, an opening for some reflection and exploration.

What would be the worst choice your child could make in life? Encourage conversation around the topic, and listen carefully to what people say. Drugs is, in my experience, the most common answer, understandably. But listen out for how they are expressing themselves and maybe even for what is not said. People may well be thinking about their own choices in life. They may also begin to think about how they, as parents or guardians, will control and influence the choices their children will make.

The questions throughout the course become increasingly personal; we could be treading on some very sensitive or private ground, so as always, avoid judgement or challenge; it's about listening, staying open-minded and affirming.

Tent/den

Some LED tealights have clever tricks, for example they 'extinguish' if you blow them or tap them or make a noise. They also can 'relight' if you repeat the action. As you and the carers are talking about child-rearing matters, the idea is to keep the babes focused on the lights.

You could do an action where you make the tent really dark, turn all the lights off for a few seconds and then turn them on again simultaneously. Notice how the babies are drawn towards the glow. When you or the tots have had enough of twinkling lights, climb out of the den and wait until the other group is ready to exit the bathing activity.

Baby bath

Negotiate with group two to see if they are ready to swap over. It doesn't matter if some come out and some stay splashing. There's room enough for three poppets in each tray, so go with the flow. But if group two are all happy to go to the tent, they'll be getting dried and dressed and can head with their leader to the den. Follow tent/den guidelines above.

Get babies undressed down to their nappies. It's fine and realistically best for everyone's health and happiness to keep nappies on while in the water trays. They do balloon up with the amount of water that they absorb (the nappies, not the babies that is) and end up weighing almost as much as the babies.

Make sure the temperature of the water is OK. It might have cooled by now. Plop babes into the water and proffer a sponge or plastic shell.

Start by singing a song or two.

Songs for the bath

Again any songs to do with water are fine. These work quite well: 'Row, row, row your boat'; there are actions and splashing involved here. '5 little ducks went swimming one day' – you might source some rubber ducks to accompany this song.

Question for carers

After one or two songs, ask the second question: 'What would be the best choice your child could make in life?' This question is harder to answer than the first. If you ask it first, you may find that parents simply answer in the negative; for example: 'not to do drugs'. By posing it at this point, it is harder to repeat an answer given for question one. Give people time to reply. It is not an easy question. Again listen carefully and respectfully to answers and store them in your mind. One mum once said she was hoping her son would become friends with her own friends' children; she felt that in this way they would grow up together and he might be influenced by them and their parents. She felt this was good because they thought in the same way as her. When I picked up on this later in the session, I spoke about community, shared values and shared responsibility.

Song/bathing

Maybe sing another song at this point or play with the babies in the bath. End the activity when babies get tired or cold.

Coffee break

It must be time for a cup of something by now. Both groups will probably have finished playing, so gather back together. This is the time for dressing babies, taking photos, playing with other babies, biscuits and coffee.

Book

When all are rested and refreshed, get out the *God Knows All About Me* books. Sit around with babes on laps and read together. I chose this book because at one point it tackles contrasting choices: 'when I'm good, when I'm bad'. I also read the following review from the bookseller's website:

We love this book ... my 9-month-old has had it read to him every night since he got it at about 7 months and he loves it, he gets all excited when it comes out. It's a big size which helps and the pictures are lovely. The rhyme is great and fun to read coz you can use funny voices for different bits. It's a lovely sentiment too and suggests an everyday and caring relationship with God. We're not very religious people, but I really like it.[44]

Comment

Talk about the session's connection with baptism or christening. Note how the babies in the blackout tent or den turned towards the light; they grabbed the holders and clung onto them. This can be understood as a picture of how we yearn towards the goodness of God. There is a rebellious side to us all; a tendency to turn to something we know isn't good for us, but we also have a choice to turn back to what is right, to God. In the baptism, the vicar will say: 'God calls us out of darkness into his marvellous light.' The light in baptism symbolizes the Christian beliefs about Jesus being the light of the world. 'Jesus spoke to them, saying, "I am the light of the world. Whoever follows me will never walk in darkness but will have the light of life"' (John 8.12).

You probably don't need to say much more than this. At this point in the session the little ones are getting tired, so you may not have more than a sentence or two, but the key points are:

- baptism is a choice you are making for your child
- you are deciding that s/he will turn from darkness or wrong things towards the light and love of God: towards all that is right and good and promotes their flourishing.

Song

'The Spirit lives to set us free' is perfect for this session for obvious reasons! 'We are marching in the light of God' is another good song to use. We use it again in the last session, Storytime, so it's worth teaching. My experience is that most non-church people don't know it. You can do some clapping or stamping of feet.

---

44 www.amazon.co.uk/God-Knows-All-About-Me/dp/1860246958/ref=sr_1_1?s=books &ie=UTF8&qid=1385474843&sr=1-1&keywords=god+knows+all+about+me

Baby record book and post-its

Hand out some post-its. Encourage carers to write down the best choices their child could make in life. This may also be a point to pick up on some of the comments proffered earlier and suggest a theological reflection of it. For example, if a mum talks about her child choosing to follow a role-model, you could talk about Jesus being the role-model for church communities.

Suggest the carers turn their choice into a prayer: 'Dear God I pray that George at moments of difficulty chooses the right people for advice and help.'

Song

'He's got the whole world in his hands' as in previous weeks.

Handouts!

Don't forget handouts.

Notices about the following week

Tell everyone that next week we'll be looking at prayer and using bubbles. Ask them if anyone else is coming for the last session on the Saturday – dads, partners, or godparents. It's useful for you to have an idea of numbers.

Blessing

Choose a suitable blessing or a short prayer – for example, the grace – to finish.

As for previous sessions, help carers and clear up. Wipe the changing mats down with the antibacterial wipes. Pack away all the Splash! things, except for the shallower cement mixer tray which will be needed for Storytime. Everything else can be stored until the next course.

Session 4: Bubble-Talk

'Lord, teach us to pray.'
(Luke 11.1)

Why Bubble-Talk? A theological reflection

People understand prayer and practise prayer in a variety of ways. In this reflection, I put forward my own understanding which relies heavily on Paul's in his letter to the Romans:

> Likewise the Spirit helps us in our weakness; for we do not know how to pray as we ought, but that very Spirit intercedes with sighs too deep for words. And God, who searches the heart, knows what is the mind of the Spirit, because the Spirit intercedes for the saints according to the will of God. (Romans 8.26–27)

A few years ago, I heard a sermon that explained what we do when we come to prayer. The vicar talked about placing yourself intentionally in a position to receive God. In doing so, you are joining others all doing the same. This forms a kind of connecting 'tunnel' between God and his creation. When I conflated the Romans passage with this sermon, an image came to mind, which is used in the handout for this session:

One way to imagine prayer is the feeling of talking to someone when you're underwater and they are above you. You have put yourself in a slightly unfamiliar environment; you want to express something and the words come out as effervescing bubbles; you can't see the person above the water clearly, but you know he's there and that somehow he understands exactly what your 'bubble-talk' intended to say.

One of the play-metaphor games we do in this session is to have babies lying on the floor while a large piece of blue (reminiscent of water) material 'floats' over the top and moves up and down. The beach balls (our prayer-bubbles) roll around over the top and the babies see the silhouette of their movement. It gives a sense of being 'underwater' and prayer rolling around us.

You may have used bubbles in your own church as part of the inter-cessions; they rise up 'like incense' (Psalm 141.2).

The second game or play-metaphor developed in an intriguing way. We play with all sorts of toy, soft balls rolling around while music is played. When the music stops, we stop rolling the balls around. (I borrowed this from a Sure Start group.) I used it to illustrate how prayer can involve words, liturgy, 'noise' as exemplified by the music and movement of the balls, but we should also try to stop, to still ourselves before God to listen: 'children can be helped to see that ... there may be important periods of waiting, silence and stillness where you don't know what might happen next'.[45] This continues to be part of the theological rationale behind it.

However, after I had done this session a couple of times, it dawned on me (or did God reveal it?) that this was a brilliant illustration of how God responds in prayer. We push up prayers to God; our prayer takes a certain form and we often have a clear expectation of what form the answer should take and from which direction it should travel back. However, God often replies in ways we don't expect: the answer returns in a completely different form and from a completely different angle.

---

45 Rebecca Nye, *Children's Spirituality*, London: Church House Publishing, 2009, p. 60.

Aims for this session

The main aim of Bubble-Talk is:

- to encourage parents to pray and for them in turn to encourage their children to pray.

We do this by:

- reflecting on the differences between human communication, verbal and non-verbal, and our interaction with God

- beginning to explain how to pray and what to expect

- broaching the idea that silence and stillness is part of prayer.

What you need

For this session you will need your two Bubble-Talk boxes, containing:

- 10 copies of 'Speak to me in Bubbles'
- Other 'bubble' books
- Large piece of blue material
- 9 bottles bubble mixture
- CD of children's music
- CD player or other music-playing device
- Various toy balls
- 1 large beach ball
- Small beach balls
- Handouts

Extra setting up

Even with a car tyre inflator plugged into the mains of my car, it still takes at least twenty minutes to blow up the large beach ball. The smaller ones take about five minutes each.

Health and safety for Bubble-Talk

Size of the balls

The balls that we use should be a variety of sizes and colours, but none should be smaller than a satsuma.

Bubble mixture

The carers use a bottle of bubble mixture to blow bubbles for their babies. They are responsible for making sure that their infants do not ingest the mixture and that they do not drip bubble liquid into eyes. If there are any spillages, mop them up quickly to avoid anyone slipping.

How to run the Bubble-Talk session

Session overview

Songs: 'Hello everyone, how are you?'
            'Clap your hands'
            '1,2,3, Jesus loves me' (*suggestion*)

Recap of last three sessions.

Q: Favourite non-verbal communication with your baby?

Songs: 'What shall we do with a bouncing baby?'
            'The little green frog'
            'Round and round the garden'

Activity: Blowing bubbles to our children.

Q: How does your baby communicate with you?
   The way God communicates with us is not the same as one human being talking to another using words and body language.

Read: 'Speak to me in bubbles' books

Songs: 'Pat-a-cake'
               'Wind the bobbin up'

Activity: Blue material with beach balls

Songs: 'My Bonnie lies over the ocean' *or*
               'The big ship sailed on the Ally-Ally-Oh'
               'With Jesus in the boat' (*suggestion*)

Activity: Musical soft ball play with music.

This interaction between us, using these toy balls, is a bit like prayer. When we pray we throw up some words, but the response maybe comes back at an angle or in an unexpected way. But also silence and stillness are important too.

Baby record book

Prayer with children; post-its. Homework at end of the day! One good thing; one thing you and baby struggled with today.

Song: 'He's got the whole world in his hands'

Handouts!

Saturday session: Storytime, about reading Bible stories.
Again: numbers for Saturday morning.

Blessing

Detailed description of the Bubble-Talk session

Invite carers to lay their towel down (if they've brought one – this is not so necessary for this session) on the changing mat underneath baby.

Songs and introductions

Once everyone has gathered and settled, start with the regular songs; for us: 'Hello everyone, how are you?', 'Clap your hands' and '1,2,3, Jesus love me'.

Recap on the last three sessions: Peek-a-Boo!, where we talked about explaining God; How Much Love?, which was about the love we give and God's love for us, and Splash! where we looked at baptism and thinking about positive choices. Ask if anyone wants to say anything or ask any questions. Remind everyone that you're available to talk at any point during or after the session.

Introduce this week's session, Bubble-Talk. I say something like:

Today, we'll be discussing prayer and illustrating it through our activities. It may feel weird to talk about prayer, but a lot of people apparently do pray and that includes children, though they rarely admit to it.

Question for carers

As we are broaching the idea of communicating with God, this week's questions focus on different forms of communication. We start with: 'What is your favourite non-verbal communication with your baby?'

You might need to give an example yourself to get the conversation started; I generally talk about blowing raspberries on my children's tummies. You'll be amazed at some of the replies! You can ask them to demonstrate their answers, where appropriate.

Songs

As there's been quite a lot of talk, it's good to sing some songs at this point. 'What shall we do with a bouncing baby?' and 'The little green frog' are excellent because they involve non-verbal communication.

Blow bubbles

Give out the bottles of bubble mixture. Allow carers to blow bubbles with the baby sitting or lying down watching. Older infants are more responsive to this activity, but younger ones are learning to track movement with their eyes, so may have a more concentrated facial expression. Carry on for as long as it seems to interest the babies. I sometimes take photos at this point.

Question for carers

After a good few minutes of blowing bubbles, you could ask the question about how carers feel their baby communicates with them? You can listen to answers while they carry on blowing bubbles or after they've finished that activity.

Comment

Just a quick comment at this point, along the lines of:

> We've been talking about how we communicate with our little ones and it's not the same as one adult talking to another. The way God communicates with us is not the same as one person talking to another using words and body language.

Participants may well be thinking 'well, what is it like then?' They'll have to wait for the next part of the session. If the bubble mixture has worn out its attraction, collect up the bottles and tidy away.

Book

Hand out the 'Speak to me in bubbles' books. Ensure babies can see the book sitting with their mums/carers. A short explanation behind this book:

People say all sorts of things to babies, don't they? When my daughter was a baby, babbling away, while I was waiting at bus-stops or after church, women would often stop by her pram and speak to her. A common remark was: are you telling a story? Go on, tell me your story. Initially I was struck by the fact that these lovely ladies *listened* to what I might at the time have described as 'drivel'. They honoured it with their attention and response, which was sometimes verbal, sometimes not. Thinking about this over time has made me realize this desire to tell, to confide our 'story', is crucial to our well-being. I believe God invites us to tell him our story daily and this is called prayer. Like my daughter's babbling, prayer does not have to be offered in the form of words. I end the book with the line 'and if you must, use words' partly because I want to honour the role that non-verbal communication plays especially between an infant and their principal carer, but partly because the phrase borrows from a quote that may or may not have originated with Francis of Assisi: 'preach the gospel, and if necessary, use words'. The point here is that God's relationship with us may not primarily be shared with us through a formalized language structure.

Read the book through twice and explain that the person talking to the child could be a parent, but could equally be God.

Songs

This is a good time to sing more songs. I've put down 'Pat-a-cake' and 'Wind the bobbin up' but any will do really.

Material and beach or soft balls

Clear the central area of debris: books, bubble mixture, tissue boxes, wipes. Ask the carers to lay their babies down on the rug/blanket. You can lay them side by side in a row or in a horseshoe arrangement. They should be able to reach out and touch their adjacent baby friend. It's best if they're not too close because they can grab hair, scratch or wallop their neighbours, albeit unintentionally. The carers sit or kneel close by, at their feet. Make sure the babies can see their carers. Take the large piece of blue Lycra or voile; ask the carers to grab hold of an edge; they will stretch the material across the top of the prostrate babies. If you know parachute games, it works a bit like this, except with babies underneath. Lift the material up and down gently; not smothering the tots! Allow them to get used to this. Then lob some beach balls over the top of the material and make them roll around. The babies will see the silhouette of the balls moving across the material. Sing some songs – see below.

Note: In our experience, some babies vehemently object to this activity. They may feel claustrophobic or abandoned by their carers, or that the sky is falling down! If so, get their carers to lift them onto their knees and allow them to see what is going on 'above'. Some babies think it's hilarious or are completely mesmerized. Curtail the activity if it's not working and have a break; go with the flow!

Songs

We sing some of the verses (all of them makes it rather long) of 'My Bonnie lies over the ocean' or 'The big ship sailed on the Ally-Ally-Oh' while we are moving the balls over the material.

Coffee break

It must be time for a break! Collect up and pack away the blue material.

Musical soft ball play

While the coffee break is happening, get the CD player plugged in, if it's not already. You will need an assistant to help pause and start the music. When everyone's refreshed and ready, get out all the balls you have. Place them in the central area. The babies can start to play with them. Get the participant adults to sit in a tight circle around the central area, with babies inside the circle, preferably on their laps. You need to be part of the circle as well. The game is to roll the balls around the group; as soon as a ball comes near to you, you push it back to another part of the circle. Everyone does this while the music plays. The assistant leader pauses the music from time to time, like in musical chairs or pass the parcel; when s/he does this, the balls should remain still. You hold onto a ball if you have one and wait until the music starts again. Allow the babies to push, roll, pat, bat the balls as much as possible but try to encourage stillness when the music stops. Do this for a while.

Comment

This interaction between us, using these toy balls, is a bit like prayer. When we pray we throw up some words, but the response maybe comes back at an angle or in an unexpected way – perhaps we pray that our baby sleeps; instead maybe a friend offers to look after her for an afternoon while you get some rest. The silence and stillness are important for understanding that prayer also involves waiting and listening.

Baby record book and post-its

Write down your favourite way of interacting with your baby. Encourage parents/carers also to try and pray with their baby this evening. Think through one good thing about the day and one part of the day where you and your baby struggled. Talk to God about those two things and end with Amen.

Song

'He's got the whole world in his hands'

Handouts

Don't forget!

Notices about the following week

Next session is on Saturday. It is good to find out who is coming, especially if there are siblings who will need childcare.

Blessing

End with your blessing or prayer.

As for previous sessions, help carers and clear up. Wipe the changing mats down with the antibacterial wipes. Pack away all the Bubble-Talk things, except for the large piece of blue material, which will be used in the following session, Storytime. Everything else can be stored until the next course.

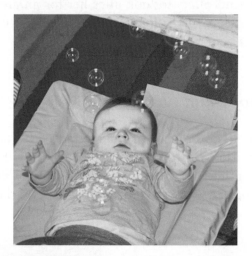

Session 5: Storytime

Then beginning with Moses and all the prophets, he interpreted to them the things about himself in all the scriptures.

(Luke 24.27)

Why Storytime? A theological reflection

There are three stories enacted in Storytime: The Lost Sheep, The Wise and Foolish Builders and Exodus. Why these three in particular? The main reasons are as follows:

- First, they are all very easy to act out and they lend themselves to multi-sensory elements; much of the action is visual, tactile and involves appropriate songs.
- Second, they are relatively simple to follow, yet, as with many biblical tales, also subtle and profound.
- The two parables are stories that families can relate to:
  - If you lost your child, you would not give up looking for them.
  - What sort of 'rocks' or values do you want your child to rely on as they grow up?
  (see the comments given during the session).
- Earlier I mentioned that the Exodus narrative is at the root of our faith. It features in the baptism service; God commissions us to tell it to our children[46] and it connects us to something bigger – to that community of believers who have experienced a faithful relationship with God for centuries and centuries.

---

46 Deuteronomy 4.9.

You are welcome to choose other stories that you feel would work well here; the only criteria being they should be baby-focused and easily accessible to parents/carers.

What should be addressed in Storytime, however, is the *point* of reading the Bible to children. Hence the question 'why do we tell children stories?' Our experience is that parents suggest answers such as 'because it's fun' or 'it's a time together'. Occasionally, I might have someone say 'they teach a lesson'. Here we are getting closer to a sense of truth. Truth comes through stories (for example, in the handout I talk about Beauty and the Beast demonstrating that looks are not everything). This sort of truth has as much validity as a scientific axiom. But the Bible doesn't stop with truths concerning instruction and information; it invites people to go beyond, to enter into a living knowledge of God in their lives today: 'a story always evokes a response. It takes us up into it, and it is not possible to read or hear a story without it impinging on our own story, or even becoming our story'.[47]

Aims for this session

The main aim of Storytime is:

- to give parents/carers the confidence to pick up Bible stories and read them to their children.

Other aims:

- to draw attention to the many levels or layers associated with Bible stories

- to give pointers on how to interpret or reflect on biblical narrative

- to emphasize the great benefits of telling these stories over and over again.

---

47 John Drane, *The McDonaldization of the Church*, London: Darton, Longman and Todd, 2000, p. 140.

What you need

For this session you will need your two Storytime boxes, containing:

- Large cushion or pillow
- Farm-animal print and green material
- Toy sheep
- Pebbles
- Large plastic, but sturdy, jug
- Red and grey material
- Large blue material
- 'Moses'/shepherd doll
- Range of children's Bible stories
- Handouts
- Evaluation/Feedback forms[48]
- *Large bag of sand*
- *Cement mixer trays*

The last two items will not fit into the boxes, but are also part of this session.

Extra setting up

Display your Bible books

Children's and especially baby books are best experienced in the flesh as it were. Baby books often encourage touch and movement; cut-out patches allow different textures to be explored (see the *That's Not My ...* range); others have flaps to open. You can't do this on www.amazon.co.uk. If you talk to your local Christian resource centre or bookshop, they may agree to a sale or return arrangement. The shorter the period you take the books away from the store, the more likely they are to agree. That way, you can show how the baby Bibles work, with their flaps and turning shutter-like pictures. Bring a good range of tomes, covering a wide age-range. The people who attend this course are not likely to actively seek out Christian bookshops, so you need to bring it to them. Make an attractive display or use a children's bookshelf, where you can see the front of the books.

---

48 On the accompanying CD.

Central area

For this session, unlike the others, don't put out the wipes and tissues in the centre of the room. This space is needed as a sort of stage/platform. The story action happens here, so leave any spare items on the table at the back.

The dad dynamic

Generally speaking the extra adults who come to this session are the dads, but you may have another family member or a close godparent. It's good to know more or less who belongs to which baby. It changes the dynamics quite significantly having (a) often double the number of adults and (b) a male presence. I have had one dad who came to some of the rest of the course, but generally speaking it's an all-female environment up to this final session. I may be throwing my political correctness caution to the winds here when I say my impression is that mums are more relaxed and less inhibited about singing, joining in the activities, being or looking 'silly' in front of others than are the dads. Be as welcoming and friendly as possible; assure them that all we do is for their child's benefit. Make two points really clear:

- The more they join in today and carry on some of the activities at home, the better it is for their baby.
- What we talk about in the course involves them as much as it does mum.

The mums do want their partners involved. At one of the Storytime sessions, one of the babies was asleep. His mum and dad were sitting in the group and the mum said, 'Can we sing that particular song later after M has woken up, because I really want T (dad) to see how we do it?' This is the only opportunity for dads to see what it's all about; they and you should make the most of it.

Health and safety for Storytime

Pebbles or stones

The pebbles will be picked up and gnawed by babies. The smallest one needs to be approximately the size of a satsuma, so they can't be swallowed.

Sand

When people's houses get flooded, they call in the army to toss sandbags around. Note the use of young lads at the peak of physical fitness here. Bags of sand are not for the faint-hearted and especially not for the weak-hearted. It would be best if two people carried the bag. You'll find out why when you try and shift it by yourself.

How to run the Storytime session

Session overview

Songs: 'Hello everyone, how are you?'
          'Clap your hands'
          '1,2,3, Jesus loves me' (*suggestion*)

Recap on previous topics.

Today we're talking about stories.

Challenge! Call out some children's stories or nursery stories. Try telling the story to your partner/or neighbour.

Q: Why do we tell children stories?

Stories

Songs: 'Little Bo Peep has lost her sheep'
          'Baa, baa, black sheep'

Stories for children need to be repeated because they accept they do not understand straight away.

Story 1 – The Lost Sheep (lots of sheep; green bushes, etc.)
Story 2 – The Wise and Foolish Builders (tray with sand and rocks)

Song: 'The wise man built his house upon the rock'

Any answers? Q
Stories are for entertaining and for teaching lessons in life. Religious or Bible stories begin to teach us how to make sense of life. They are not always easy to understand immediately; sometimes the understanding or meaning only becomes clear when we actually experience something that makes us identify with a particular character in one of the stories. It becomes part of our story.

Story 3 – Exodus

Songs: 'We are marching in the light of God (*suggestion*). If your church does not have permission to use this song, try 'The Spirit lives to set us free' as an alternative.
'How did Moses cross the Red Sea?'

Baptism story liturgy:
Over water the Holy Spirit moved in the beginning of creation.
Through water you led the children of Israel from slavery in Egypt to freedom in the Promised Land.

Song: 'He's got the whole world in his hands'

Handouts and photos!

Big thanks to leaders/helpers

Blessing

Make sure everyone fills out a feedback form

Mention other child-friendly activities run by the church

Detailed description of the Storytime session

Settle everyone in.

Songs and introductions

As there are 'new' people in the Storytime session, explain a bit about the course so far. Explain that what we do is for the benefit of the baby; it may bring the carers slightly out of their comfort zone, but babies long for their nearest and dearest to interact with them. During the songs, dads/other principal carers may well want to hold their tot, so do go over the actions we normally do, so they can join in fully.

Begin as always with your regular songs: 'Hello everyone, how are you?', 'Clap your hands', '1,2,3, Jesus loves me'.

Talk briefly but clearly about the first four sessions. For example:

In our first session, Peek-a-Boo!, we sang lots of peek-a-boo songs and played with material. This was to illustrate that we don't 'see' God all the time in a physical way, but people do talk about having a deep and powerful sense of God at particular moments in their lives.

In How Much Love? we did some baby touch, looked at God's love for us and our love for our children.

In Splash! we played around in a bath and lit tealights in a blackout tent. We talked about baptism or christening and what difference it makes in our lives.

Bubble-Talk focused on prayer. Communicating with God can feel strange, but prayer is simply a way of expressing your worries, your thoughts, your feelings to someone who you trust because they understand you fully.

Invite people to talk to you at any point about anything that arises from the course. Explain that today's session is all about stories; Bible stories in particular.

Challenge and question for carers

This isn't so much a question as a challenge! Tell everyone you're going to list several nursery or fairy stories. They have to choose one and tell the story as best they can to their partner and baby. They only have one minute to do this – simply due to time constraints and the fact that we don't want to take the focus away from the little ones for long. Just point out that we're not aiming to spend too long on this.

Here's a by no means exhaustive list:

Goldilocks and the Three Bears
Sleeping Beauty
Rumpelstiltskin
Cinderella
Little Red Riding Hood
Rapunzel
The Ugly Duckling
Jack and the Beanstalk
Dick Whittington
The Three Little Pigs

You could briefly ask how it felt doing that exercise.

The next question is not to be answered straight away: Why do we tell children stories? Say you'll seek their answers later on in the session. This gives everyone time to think about the question.

Songs

In preparation for the first story, sing 'Little Bo Peep has lost her sheep' and 'Baa, Baa, black sheep'.

Comment

Just say: 'Stories for children need to be repeated because they accept they do not understand straight away.'

This is partly because there is a lot of repetition in the Lost Sheep story and adults may get slightly impatient and may not realize that small children can't take ideas on board immediately. But it is also because, as we know, Bible stories often need to be read at different times of our lives in different circumstances before the truth of them takes shape and meaning for us. Biblical narratives themselves often present the reader with an awful lot of repetition, which contemporary secular society may find puzzling.[49]

Story 1: The Lost Sheep

For this story, you will need:

All the toy sheep
The farm-animal print material
The green material
The blue material
The cushion or pillow
The shepherd doll

While doing this story, you move down the room a bit, but try to keep relatively near to the babies even at the end of the story, when the shepherd has travelled a certain distance to find the sheep. If you are too far away the babies can't see the shepherd and lose interest.

One way to avoid this is to gather the babies a bit more towards the middle of the room, like a tight-knit audience, but allow yourself space to lay out the material.

Give one sheep per child (if there are brothers and sisters in this session, give them a sheep as well if they want one). Keep one sheep yourself. Put any spare sheep away back in the box. Get the 'Moses'/shepherd doll, the farm animal, blue and green material and the large cushion ready beside you.

Start to read the story (in **bold**) [actions are in brackets]. There is a vague element of Godly Play in the telling of this story; if you are trained to do Godly Play, you can do your own version of this.

Once upon a time, there was a shepherd who had a flock of sheep. [Show the shepherd in one hand, keeping the sheep in the other.]

---

49 For more on this and on understanding Scripture as story, see Robert Alter, *The Art of Biblical Narrative*, New York: Basic Books, 1981, pp. 88–113.

They lived on a farm. [Lay out the farm-animal material at one end of the central blanket/rug, nearest the babies.]

Every morning the shepherd counted the sheep; 1, 2, 3 ... [Go round with the shepherd counting the sheep; get all the adults to join in the counting. It doesn't matter if one or two sheep get pushed out of sight, but do just stick to one final number.]

Afterwards, he took the sheep to the field. The sheep ate the green, green grass. [Lay out the green piece of material a little bit further down the central area and make your sheep 'nibble' the 'grass'.]

In the afternoon, the sheep went back to the farm. [Move back to the farm and place your sheep there.]

Every evening, the shepherd counted the sheep, 1, 2, 3 ... [Count everyone's sheep again.]

One morning the shepherd counted the sheep, 1, 2, 3 ... [Count everyone's sheep again.]

He took them to the field and they ate the green, green, grass. [Place your sheep on the green material.]

One of the sheep started to wander away. [Move your sheep away from the babies and place it behind the cushion.]

Where's the sheep?

Behind the hill.

He started to wander further away. I wonder why he started to go away. [Move the sheep further away still and lay down the blue material in the shape of a river. Place the sheep in the river.]

Where's the sheep?

He's in the river.

He wandered even further away. I wonder why is he doing that? [Move him further away, even out of sight.]

Where's the sheep?

In the afternoon, the shepherd took the sheep to the farm. [Move all the way back to the farm material.]

In the evening, he counted the sheep, 1, 2, 3 ... [Count everyone's sheep again, which should be one short of your final number.]

Huh? One of the sheep is missing.

The shepherd started to look for the sheep. [Move the shepherd to the green material.]

Is he in the field? ... No. [Move the shepherd to the cushion.]

Is he behind the hill? ... No. [Move the shepherd to the blue material.]

Is he in the river? ... No.

I wonder why the shepherd kept looking for the sheep. [Move the shepherd to the place where the sheep is.]
Ah look, the sheep is in the brambles. The shepherd rescues the sheep. He and the sheep are very happy. [Make the shepherd hold the sheep and carry it back to the farm. Smile lots.]

Gather up the material, the sheep and the shepherd and put away. This also allows people and babies to have a pause, chat, feed, nappies, etc.

Story 2: The Wise and Foolish Builders

For this story, you will need:

> the shallower of the two cement mixer trays
> the bag of play sand
> a large plastic, but strong, scooping jug
> lots of pebbles

Place the cement mixer tray in the central area. Gather all the babies around the edge of the tray. Get parents to take off their shoes, socks, baby booties, tights and other miscellaneous footgear. Babies can sit in the tray or on their parents' knees with their feet dangling well into the tray.

Tip out all the pebbles into the middle of the tray, obviously avoiding tots' toes. It's good to have lots – both for babes and adults. I try and keep the heaviest ones myself, as these are hard for babies to hold. Offer the stones to the children and invite adults to help themselves. Remind parents to check their babies cannot swallow the pebble. Allow a bit of time for babies to explore and feel the stones; there's something inexpressibly soothing about a smooth, mottled pebble.

Song

Whip out the Song Book and turn to 'The wise man built his house'. As you sing verse 1, knock your pebbles together in beat to the music. Do the actions for the rain coming down, etc.

You will have to pause briefly before carrying on to the next part of the song.

Leave the pebbles with the babies or in the tray. Grab your jug, and the play sand (dads may come in handy for moving the bag of sand nearer to you). Scoop up a goodly quantity of sand in the jug.

Sing the second verse. As you sing 'The foolish man built his house upon the sand', slowly pour the sand over the feet and toes of the babies. Do the actions for the chorus.

Repeat the whole song and action together again.

Allow for some free play in the sand and rocks.

Question for carers

If the children are happy milling around in the sand, elicit some answers to the question 'Why do we tell children stories?'

Naturally the carers who have been attending throughout the course feel more comfortable answering in the group than the new adults who may not know anyone else. If dads do reply, all the better.

Coffee break

This may be a good time for a break or after the comment below. Play it by ear. Whenever you do have the break, encourage people to look at the children's Bible stories displayed. Even picking up books yourself and taking them to the families to look at is a good thing to do. This could also be a good time to ask everyone to fill out their feedback form. If it's not a good time, make sure there is time to do this at the end.

Comment

My patter here goes something like:

Stories are for entertaining and for teaching lessons in life – such as, don't talk to or be waylaid by strangers (wolf or otherwise) in isolated places where there is no CCTV, like forests. Religious or Bible stories begin to teach us how to make sense of life. They are not always easy to understand immediately; sometimes the understanding or meaning only becomes clear when we actually experience something that makes us identify with a particular character in the story.

I find that I don't have time to say all of the below; so *either* I talk about the layers of the Lost Sheep story *or* the layers of the Wise and Foolish Builders.

Story 1 – The Lost Sheep

There are often several layers of meaning to a Bible story; so the Lost Sheep is on one level a simple story. The farmer loses a sheep, looks for her and finds her. On another, it portrays what a parent would do if they lost their child. (I give an example of a colleague whose daughter went missing one night; a friend told the mother to get some sleep, but she explained it was impossible to rest until she knew her daughter was safe.) On yet another, it demonstrates God's yearning for all those who are 'lost' in a much broader sense: for example those rejected by society; those suffering from poverty, war or illness.

Story 2 – The Wise and Foolish Builders

There are often several layers of meaning to a Bible story; so the Wise and Foolish Builders is on one level a bit of a laugh at the clownish, pantomine builder – no one would be so ridiculous as to construct on sand. On a completely different level, the story challenges the listeners; well, what do you think you should build your lives on? What are your 'rocks'? Have you thought about them? What would you like your child here to depend on to take him/her through difficulties in life?

Story 3 – Exodus

For this story, you will need:

  Red and grey material
  Large blue material
  'Moses'/shepherd doll

Ask everyone to take one piece of red or grey material. Show it clearly to the babies.

Have two helpers hold the blue material in the middle of the room. At the beginning they can sit down and keep the material spread out but still. At the right moment, they should wave it around to represent 'sea'. As this is the Saturday session, there might be some brothers and sisters around; they really enjoy this story, get them joining in.

Once upon a time there was a man called Moses. [Hold up 'Moses' doll.]
He was a shepherd too!
He looked after sheep, but he also looked after mummies, daddies, babies and big boys and girls.
A very bad king was very nasty to Moses and the mummies, daddies, babies and big boys and girls.
So God told Moses to take them away from the king. [Get everyone to stand up, mums, dads, boys, girls; babies need to be carried around facing forwards, unless they are really tiny and have to be carried face against chest.]
God led Moses and the people by appearing as a pillar of fire and a pillar of cloud. [Everyone walk around the room holding the material. People holding the blue 'sea' material can start making it billow and roll.]

Song

'We are marching in the light of God'. Not many people know this song, so you might need to sing it a couple of times to get them into the swing of it. Or you can replace it with 'The Spirit lives to set us free' [Sing while you walk around the sea in a big circle.]

[Stop walking and singing, then get everyone to wave their piece of material inwards. Make sure the babies can see.]

Song

'We are marching in the light of God'/'The Spirit lives to set us free'. [As you sing, walk around the room in the opposite direction, stop after singing it a couple of times, then repeat the action of waving their material inwards.]

[Now gather everyone at one end.]

Song

Explain that you are going to sing the following song and they can join in the chorus. This is because it is hard to pick up if you don't already know it! The chorus is easy, because it is to the tune of 'John Brown's body lies a-mouldering in the grave'.

Sing 'How did Moses cross the Red Sea?' [When you sing the words 'God blew with his wind', blow gently on your baby's face.]

[On the last line, the people holding the sea move towards each other so the material drops in the middle; as long as there is sufficient material covering the floor, they can gently shake the 'walls of water' on either side. You (and Moses doll) cross the sea; encourage everyone to follow you.]

[Get everyone to clap.]

Sit everyone down again. The material can be played with, or gathered up and put away. Have a little breather.

Comment

Talk briefly about how this story is mentioned in the baptism liturgy:

Over water the Holy Spirit moved in the beginning of creation.
Through water you led the children of Israel from slavery in Egypt to freedom in the Promised Land.

By this point in the session, I find it's enough to mention it and say something about how old this story is and how important it is for Jews and Christians.

Song

'He's got the whole world in his hands'

Handouts!

Give out this week's handout and any photos you have printed out for the families.

Thank yous

Acknowledge and thank all your helpers.

Prayer

Say a prayer of blessing or thanksgiving.

Evaluation forms

It is essential that the participants (those who have attended the whole course – mums or principal carer) fill out the evaluation forms. This kind of information is gold dust for the church. It can inform us about how best to serve the community at large. I have had people say the course is too short or they wish it was every week! We don't have the resources to do that, but it does show that people are willing to engage themselves and their families with our faith.

If they complete the forms there and then, you've got them. Don't let people 'take them away'. If anyone is away for the last session, send them a hard copy with an SAE and also email them with an online one.

Looking forward

Mention what else the church has to offer the families – mums and toddler groups, Messy Church, All-Age services, Festival services, and so on.

As in the coffee break, spend time showing some of the children's Bibles; hand them round for carers to try out with their babies.

As this is the last session, it would be good to make it clear how much you would like to keep in touch with the families, if they are happy with this. See the next chapter for ideas about this.

I also make sure that our vicar is present at the end of the last session. They can answer queries about baptism, meet the families and show that they take an interest in them.

Well done! You've just run your first Starting Rite course!

Part 3

Next steps

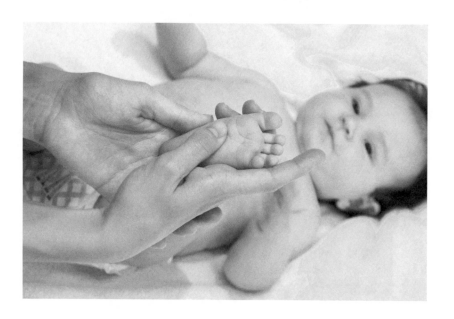

Taking it further

This final chapter is about taking the concept of Starting Rite further: taking the course further, taking the preparation for baptism further and taking the relationships you've developed with the families further. Below we look at six ways in which you can develop your Starting Rite initiative.

1. Adapting the Starting Rite course

Make it your own

As you have read through the session outline, perhaps you have thought through some other ways of conveying the ideas. Please do get your creative juices flowing! You might already have other resources; you may have a nursery that meets in your church hall and they could lend you some items, for example, some soft play equipment that would work just as well, if not better.

Just keep in mind the following:

- Use sensory (smell, touch, hearing and sight) elements as much as possible.
- Songs are always good; do use normal nursery rhymes as well as any other children's worship songs. Change the songs to ones you prefer. Make sure you observe copyright law in reproducing the songs you choose. Not all nursery rhymes are in the public domain.
- Baby health and safety is paramount. Ensure you are well-informed about what is appropriate for babies to do or experience. Your health visitors are crucial for this. They should be able to direct you to literature – online or otherwise – that can keep you up to date. For example, I have left the

sense of taste out because the World Health Organization recommends that babies under six months are fed on breast or formula milk.[50] You can however, use the *smell* of food – for example, the smell of fresh bread.

Optional Bible story for each session

Not so long ago, we had a mum who was a curate from a neighbouring diocese. She attended with her daughter and, after the course had ended, gave me some useful feedback and a very specific idea for taking Starting Rite further. Her suggestion was to include a Bible story for *all* the sessions not just in Storytime. I haven't tried this out, but the idea is certainly worth exploring as an alternative or in addition to part of the sessions.

Stories can take a lot of time, so be aware you may have to readjust your timing in the sessions.

Choose any stories you prefer that connect to the topic of the session; these are only the ones that sprang to my mind:

Peek-a-Boo!   The man born blind (John 9) *or* The road to Emmaus (Luke 24.13–35).

How Much Love?   The anointing of David (1 Samuel 16.1–13) *or* The woman anointing Jesus' feet (Luke 7.36–50).

Splash!   Moses' basket (Exodus 2.1–10) *or* Jesus' baptism (Matthew 3.13–17) *or* The calling of Zacchaeus (Luke 19.1–10) *or* Paul's conversion (Acts 9.1–22).

Bubble-Talk   Jonah praying (Jonah 1.15–end of chapter 2) *or* Jesus calming the storm (Mark 4.35–41).

2. An extra session – baptism preparation evening

At the time of writing, Starting Rite has been running for three years in our church; we offer it to any family who is interested, not just to baptism families, and it would be unrealistic to insist that all baptism families come on the course. We do, however, invite all the families who are interested

---

50 www.who.int/nutrition/topics/infantfeeding_recommendation/en/

in having their child christened to a baptism preparation evening. This has been developed by our Children and Families Lay Minister, Alison White. I explain how it works in detail below, but in short the evening covers:

- some questions about baptism
- a (physical) walk-through of the service
- some of the elements from the Starting Rite course
- any paperwork that needs to be completed for the registers (names, date of birth, godparents, etc.).

This session takes place in our church building. If you decide to do this evening, make sure it is warm enough for babies!

For this session, you will need:

- Enough copies for all participants of an outline of the evening, showing the baptism promises and the vows.
- Some A4 or A3 colour pictures of how water is used. These need to be displayed around the font area.
- Some A4 or A3 colour pictures of biblical stories about water, especially those mentioned in the baptism service. These need to be displayed around the font area.
- Enough pens and paper for all the participants.
- The objects that you use for baptism; these might include: a shell, oil, a jug used to pour water into the font, the Pascal candle and two or three baptism candles, the baptism register.
- A few toys to keep babies entertained.

Detailed description of the baptism preparation evening

Welcome

Alison starts by welcoming everyone and explaining that this evening is an opportunity to explore baptism and think about the key elements of the service. The sheets explaining the order of the evening and other information can be given out here.

She invites everyone to introduce themselves and their baby/child and say when their baptism will take place. In our group context, we also find out which church they'll be baptized in. An important point to raise early on is that christening and baptism is the same thing, so no confusion arises through the evening.

She moves on to explain the order of the evening:

- most of the time will be spent looking at the **key elements of the baptism service**
- this will be followed by **refreshments**
- during coffee, our baptism liaison people will help complete **paperwork** and families can take time to look at **children's Bibles** and the church
- families can raise questions at any time.

The baptism service

Alison starts by introducing what baptism means. She says something along the lines of:

> When we bring our children for baptism, as parents and godparents we are beginning their faith journey with them, we are making a public commitment to bring them up within Christian values, to know God and his love for them.

Question about godparents

Research done by the Church of England revealed that godparents hold a hugely important place in the eyes of the parents. So Alison's first question to the families is: how did you decide on your godparents?

The last group we had involved nine families and there were over twenty people at the evening, so we encouraged discussion in smaller groups before hearing their reasons in the whole group. If you have a gathering of six people altogether, you could probably just go round each person or couple sharing with the whole group.

The promises

Alison reads the baptism promises out. She invites them in groups of three to four to look at the promises together, and talk about what they mean.

Question about the promises

'What *practical* things might you do to fulfil these promises?' Give out the pens and paper to list some answers.

At this point, you can invite people to share some answers. People might feel a little shy about this, so here are some ideas that we suggest:

Praying for and praying with children

Alison talks about how to pray. Her way of explaining it goes something like this:

> There is no special formula to praying; we are talking to God and nothing is too trivial for him to listen to, he loves to hear from us. You can be saying thank you, sorry, asking for something. It doesn't have to be complicated, for example: 'God, I'm worried about Joe settling in at school, he is so shy and doesn't know many children.' Or it might be: 'Thank you, God, for Holly's beautiful smile ...' Prayer can be simple.

Teaching Christian values

We point parents to how to follow Jesus. For example:

- talk to your child about God; be open about your own faith – don't shy away from talking about God in everyday life situations
- answer their questions about God and if you get stuck come and see us – we might not always have the answers but we will try to help!
- your care for your children and your love for them demonstrate God's love and point to his unconditional love
- tell or read them stories from the Bible. You can pick up the question from the Storytime session: 'why do we tell stories?' Listen to the parents'

answers and incorporate those answers into how Bible stories have meaning and relevance to our lives. Point out that Bible stories also present a great way of teaching children about God's love, who Jesus is and Christian values.

Coming to church

This is an opportunity to encourage families to be involved in church and learn more about Jesus. We tell them about all the activities we do for and with children in our group of churches: toddler services, Messy Church, All Age Worship, Junior Church, Junior Choir, festival services, etc.

As part of this conversation about promises that the parents and the godparents make, Alison also makes it clear (possibly because she's been asked this question in the past) that godparents are not promising to look after the child if anything happens to the parents.

The baptism vows

Here Alison explains that in the service everyone is invited to join in but parents and the godparents must make these vows.

She then takes these vows one by one and explains them in language that is a bit more accessible.

Do you turn to Christ? Do you accept Jesus as the son of God who died for all the wrongs humankind do and rose to life again? Do you want to turn to what is right and good and for the benefit of everyone?

Do you repent of your sins? Do you accept that none of us are perfect? That we all make mistakes? Do you feel bad or sorry?

Do you renounce evil? Do you dislike or hate what is bad or wrong in the world? Drugs, violence, war; this helps to explain what we mean when we say 'do you renounce evil?' – you're saying you don't like the bad things in our world.

We don't demand answers at this point! This is more an explanation of what the questions mean, so that the parents and godparents at least feel they understand what they are agreeing with!

The signing of the cross and use of oil

We explain to the parents that during the service the baby or candidate will be signed on the forehead with the sign of the cross.

Question

'Why do we sign with the cross?'

Alison invites answers and then if necessary adds: 'The cross is the sign of Christ and of what he suffered for us on the cross. The sign might be made with holy oil which has been blessed by the bishop during Easter week and distributed to clergy.'

We then explain that this oil is so special it is kept in an aumbry and we take the families up there to show them. We talk about how many keys are needed to access the aumbry (four in our case!), and about how holy it is; which is why the oil is placed in this 'safe' near the altar. When everyone is reseated, we pass the oil around, inviting people to make a sign of the cross in the palm of their hand.

Water and the font

Everyone now moves down to the font. Alison mentions that water is very important in our lives, we can't live without it, it sustains life.

Questions

'What do we use water for on a daily basis in our lives?' 'What does water mean to you?'

Answers can be called out then and there. The key points to draw out are ideas of purity, refreshment, cleansing and new life – and this is particularly the case in baptism.

Further question

'Can anyone think of any Bible stories where water is a prominent feature?'
   Answers may include:

- Noah
- Jesus walks on water
- Jesus calms the storm
- Moses crosses the Red Sea
- Moses in the bulrushes
- The great catch of fish – post resurrection.

Alison carries on to say how water features throughout the Bible. During the service, the water is poured into the font and then blessed by the vicar who says a prayer over it. Within that prayer are references to water at important times in the Bible. She points out the pictures around the font.

- Creation – the Holy Spirit moved over water in the beginning of creation
- Moses and the parting of the Red Sea – through water you led the children of Israel from slavery in Egypt to freedom in the Promised Land
- At Jesus' baptism – in water your son Jesus received the baptism of John and was anointed by the Holy Spirit as the Messiah, the Christ, to lead us from the death of sin to newness of life.

Light and candles

We move back to the pews and someone lights a candle on the altar. You could have a number of lighted candles and give one to each participant.

Questions

'What does a lighted candle mean to you?' 'What do we use candles for today?'
   A candle gives us light, it shows us the way. It reminds us to help the baby/candidate to walk in God's way; in the light of Christ.
   A couple of baptism candles are passed around the group to have a look at.

Paschal candle

Many people don't really understand the significance of the Paschal candle. So at this point Alison brings the candle to show everyone and explains some of the symbols. Her spiel is something like this:

> The Paschal candle is a large white candle with symbols of the cross and alpha and omega on it. A new Paschal candle is blessed and lit at Easter and is used through the Paschal or Easter season and then throughout the year on special occasions, such as baptisms. The flame of the Paschal candle symbolizes the eternal presence of Christ, light of the world in the midst of his people: he who is the second person of the Trinity, the Alpha and Omega.

You could also explain the five marks of the nails if that's an important part of your tradition and theology.

Final points about the baptism service

Alison finishes by noting we have covered the key elements of a baptism service. The service also comprises readings, a sermon, prayers, hymns and communion. She mentions that families can choose a special prayer for their child and may have a favourite hymn they would like to include in the service.

This is a time to note other points about church that may be unfamiliar to families, for example:

- we offer a Junior church, so children can go out for a large part of the service, but will obviously be invited to watch the baptism
- during the baptism, at the font, everyone from the baptism party can come and gather around the font
- how communion works in our church; you can come up for a blessing
- you could/should?! bring your newly baptized baby up for a blessing
- during the third hymn, people will come around with plates for donations, you can Gift Aid.

Any questions about the service?

We invite people to express any questions/concerns/worries they have. Our baptism liaison volunteers are available to talk with families individually, and this lessens any feelings of embarrassment. It's good to stress there are no silly questions!

Refreshments and final bits and pieces

To finish off, we offer coffee and tea and allow people to wander around the church. The baptism register is available for people to look at and see how their child's baptism will be recorded. Putting out a variety of children's Bibles is a great idea (as we do in Storytime); families and godparents can be encouraged to pick up books and take note of them. The Children's Society also offer some lovely gifts for babies, while also raising money for their fantastic work; see http://shop.childrenssociety.org.uk/gifts-vouchers/christening-gifts/

This is also the time to fill out any details for the baptism registers; volunteers from our church work through this with the families.

At the end of the last baptism preparation evening, I spoke to one mum who said that the session had made her feel more comfortable about it all. She felt that Alison had made the language 'more modern'. As she had not been able to attend Starting Rite, she was interested in getting a copy of the handout on Splash!, which I emailed to her subsequently.

3. Welcoming baptism families

While we're on the topic of the baptism service, think about how your church responds to the welcome of the families. Here are some ideas:

* What about giving a gift or card? There is an excellent book *Making the Most of Your Child's Baptism*[51] by Ally Barrett, which gives some creative ideas for parents to continue and support the faith journey. Another

---

51 Ally Barrett, *Making the Most of Your Child's Baptism*, London: SPCK, 2011.

book edited by Robert Atwell is *Gift: 100 readings for new parents*.[52] This comprises a selection of pieces from poetry, Scripture, and other literary forms.

- Remember the photos you took during the course? Could you use these on a baptism service sheet or on the screen, if your church uses one? Could you make a baptism certificate/godparents' cards with the baby's photo?
- Could you sing one of the Starting Rite songs during the baptism service? 'We are marching in the light of God' would make a good choice; it's used in Storytime, so some of the dads would have learned it and it fits in with the symbolism of the baptism candle.
- Some churches hold their baptisms after the main Sunday service – do other people from your congregation attend these? Could the Starting Rite leaders come along?

These are just a few ideas, no doubt your own church will have many more.

4. Using the evaluation forms

Initially the aim of the evaluation forms was to gauge how well Starting Rite was received. Once I had adapted the course sufficiently and it was clear people enjoyed it, the form was changed and took more of a market research approach. As it stands, the evaluation can help in both these ways.

Is the course working?

The feedback from the forms can help you assess if the course is working in the way you expect. For example, if one of your frustrations is a feeling that parents don't really understand baptism, then the forms can let you know whether carers have at least moved on in their grasp of the sacrament. If your frustration is that families show little or no serious interest in the Christian faith, beyond a 'wash and go' christening, the questions about reading the handouts may indicate whether parents have at least wanted to discover more.

---

52 Robert Atwell, *Gift: 100 readings for new parents*, Norwich: Canterbury Press, 2005.

What are your families looking for?

Second, the forms give the opportunity to gather market research information. One question asks if the course is too long or short; a few people have responded with the words 'too short; wish it was on every week'! We don't have the resources to do this, but you might! Some have suggested how to advertise the course better (and what a gift to have that kind of information!).

The final question asks 'Would you be interested in other activities run by the church?' This gives us the confidence to contact the families about further child-friendly services or events. You could adapt the form to suit your own situation. For example, if you were thinking of starting a Messy Church:

- Would you be interested in coming to a Messy Church service (with an explanation of Messy Church)?
- What day and time would suit your family?

You could ask anything that helps you to determine how to keep the relationship going; this is taken up more fully in section 6 on p. 170, 'Following up with families and welcoming them'. The evaluation forms can be found on the accompanying CD.

5. Taking the Starting Rite threads further in worship

Starting Rite helps to familiarize parents with the signs and symbols of church practice. If, as we would all hope, your families begin to attend church for worship, one way of making them feel more at home is to introduce Starting Rite practices into those services.

Songs

If you haven't attended church very often before your child's christening, going along and singing hymns that are completely unknown to you must feel awkward. Could your church try to sing some of the songs from the Starting Rite course at an All-Age service? You might have to teach the regular congregation the 'new' songs, but the Starting Rite families would be sitting pretty and smug that they had that chorus nailed already.

Using oil

Your church may already use oil for healing services. Could you use it in different ways? How about anointing children/young people as they take a new step in their lives? When they start school, primary or secondary; when they leave for university? I work as a university chaplain and they certainly need something to prepare them for the alcoholic tidal wave of Freshers' Week.

Could you give gentle hand massages as part of a healing service or during the peace?

Bubbles

Have you ever used bubbles as part of your intercessions? The idea is to pray a prayer as you blow bubbles and watch them rise up.

Lights in the darkness

If you run an after-school church group, like Messy Church or a Sunday afternoon service, you may find that in the autumn and winter months you can play around with darkness and light. I once created a blacked-out room and took a group of around twenty toddlers and carers into it to give them the sense of blindness. They weren't scared but an awed hush descended on the whole group. We then lit all the electric tealights one by one to enable our 'sight' and to show how the light shines in the darkness.

6. Following up with families and welcoming them

Recently the Church of England commissioned a research project among baptism families. The results highlight some key findings and implications for churches. This section looks at some of these implications and how your church can respond.

Taking the relationship with children further

The Church of England research showed that most families would like to keep in touch with the church (in fact, to my astonishment, nine out of ten); it recommends that:

> the church needs to be more intentional about building that connection. After making a strong start with the christening, churches should continue to nurture relationships with families.[53]

The research also highlights the barriers to church-going for people with toddlers and tots and suggests that:

> parents should be aware of what churches do to help support families with young children ... Churches also need to let parents know about other church-based activities.[54]

So, whether it's by email, your website or Facebook page, by hook or by crook let your Starting Rite families know what is hip and happening at your church. Make it clear that it is appropriate for children. When our children's and families' minister tells carers about a service, she always uses phrases like: 'child-friendly'; 'activities'; 'moving around'; 'hardly any sitting still in pews' and, in a final flourish, she emphasizes the permission to make NOISE.

Clearly it's important to advertise all the regular services and activities that are child-friendly. For example, if you have a mums and toddlers group or pram service; Junior church/Sunday school/crèche, etc.; any All-Age services or Messy Church.

---

53 *Christening Matters, Key Findings*, 9dot research, 2014, p. 6.
54 *Christening Matters*, p. 8.

There are lots of ways to welcome babies and their families at church. Here are a few we have used in our church community:

1. We offered a free lunch at the end of one course. This was a good way for some of the church regulars (who prepared and served the lunch) to meet parents and coo over babies. This means when families do come to church they recognize a few more faces.
2. When a Starting Rite baby is baptized in our church, we give them a small gift and card to recognize their past participation in the course and to honour their present and future place among us.
3. Since expanding our children's ministry in our church, we have had so many more babies coming to our toddler service that we've had to buy baby ribbon rings[55] as a way of enabling them to 'dance' to the music and singing parts of the service. This is one of the ways we encourage babies to join in the church's corporate worship.

But it's also important to bear in mind another implication from the research: 'Churches need to recognize that faith journeys do not always involve regular churchgoing.'[56] So it's also about capitalizing on forthcoming events. The Church year, its seasons and festivals come into their own here. How about your harvest festival service or Christingle or even Father's Day?[57]

Our last Starting Rite ran through Lent. This – top tip! – proved a good time to carry out the course. If this is the first child for the couple, Mothering Sunday takes on a whole new meaning, experience and attraction for the family. It also leads up to Easter, and most churches offer a family service or perhaps other children's activities around this time.

Every year we run a children-centred activity service on Good Friday. Naturally, we invited the Starting Rite group to church that day and four families out of the seven came along. It was a good time to catch up with them; one mum had been unable to make the last session, but had sent dad with baby, albeit with a heads-up to me that dad wasn't particularly enthusiastic. At the Good Friday service, she told me that dad had really enjoyed it after all. It was also great to see that a mum could come to a church service

---

55 We got ours, if you're interested, from www.bensley.clara.co.uk/
56 *Christening Matters*, p. 5.
57 Our church has in the past used: Sandra Millar, *Festivals Together: Creating all-age worship through the year*, London: SPCK, 2012. The book suggests celebrating Father's Day as a church service.

for the first time and meet up and already know a number of other friendly faces.

Taking the relationship with parents further

One of the main aims of Starting Rite is to nurture the babies' spiritual growth; but by default, the course prompts the parents to think through their own faith. The Church of England research notes that:

> Churches need to recognize the faith journeys of parents and do what they can to support and encourage them on their journey with God. Deciding to have their child christened was a significant step on their journey.[58]

Your church may already run Christian basics courses for adults and some of the Starting Rite parents might be interested in finding out more. There are plenty available: Alpha; Emmaus; Puzzling Questions; Table Talk; and Pilgrim, to name but a few. Your diocesan mission enabler or equivalent will be able to direct you to others. If you feel that the parents are not quite ready for these or if the demands of parenthood are preventing further exploration at this point, then keep the relationship going through invitation to other church events, social or otherwise.

The point, as emphasized in the Church of England research, is to maintain the contact with the family, assuring them that they belong to the Church family and, as such, they are supported and welcomed. It is no more and no less the promise we make in the baptism service:

> People of God, will you welcome these children and uphold them in their new life in Christ?

All   **With the help of God, we will.**

---

58 *Christening Matters*, p. 5.

Conclusion

Hopefully, this book will have given you the confidence and know-how to put on a Starting Rite course. If you go ahead and run one, I truly hope and pray that you will enjoy it as much as I do and that you see God at work among the families you meet.

Do you remember the questions I asked in the Introduction about your own baptism preparation (p. 9)? The last question was: 'Do you ever receive feedback or appreciation of your baptism preparation?' In answer to this, check out this comparison, drawn from my own experience:

| **Three years of running Starting Rite** – countless expressions of thanks through emails, cards, chocolates, hugs, flowers and home-made craft objects. | vs | **Four years of showing parents a baptism service sheet** – number of cards/gifts/hugs/ craft objects: 0. |

A flippant point in itself, but appreciation is the beginning of relationship; relationship is the beginning of trust, and when you have trust you may have openness, and that's when the Holy Spirit can really start to move in and among us.

In the middle of one Starting Rite course I ran, a mum sent me this in an email: '... I have really enjoyed the last 3 weeks and have reopened up a stronger feeling towards God and how to include God in the life of my children. Thank you so much for the chance to come along.'

This is what Starting Rite is all about: nudging people towards God and opening opportunities for his Holy Spirit to work and play in their lives.

Further Reading and Bibliography

Baby development

Kaz Cooke, *The Rough Guide to Babies and Toddlers*, London: Penguin, 2009 (especially pages 196–222).

Sue Gerhardt, *Why Love Matters: How Affection Shapes a Baby's Brain*, London: Brunner-Routledge, 2004.

Penelope Leach, *Your Baby and Child*, London: Dorling Kindersley, 2003.

Dr William Sears and Martha Sears, *The Baby Book*, London: Thorsons, 2005 (especially pages 464–6).

Mary Sheridan, *From Birth to Five Years: Children's Development Progress*, London: Routledge, 2007.

http://www.nhs.uk/Conditions/pregnancy-and-baby/

Children's spiritual development

John Drane and Olive M. Fleming Drane, *Family Fortunes*, London: Darton, Longman and Todd, 2004.

David Hay with Rebecca Nye, *The Spirit of the Child*, revd edn, London: Jessica Kingsley Publishers, 2006.

Nicky and Sila Lee, *The Parenting Book*, London: Alpha International, 2009.

Rebecca Nye, *Children's Spirituality: What it is and why it matters*, London: Church House Publishing, 2009.

Anne Richards and Peter Privett (eds), *Through the Eyes of a Child: New insights in theology from a child's perspective*, London: Church House Publishing, 2009.

Catherine Stonehouse and Scottie May, *Listening to Children on the Spiritual Journey*, Grand Rapids: Baker Publishing Group, 2010.

All-age worship

Sandra Millar, *Festivals Together: Creating all-age worship through the year*, London: SPCK, 2012.
Sandra Millar, *Worship Together: Creating all-age services that work*, London: SPCK, 2012.
Lucy Moore, *All Age Worship*, London: Bible Reading Fellowship, 2010.
Lucy Moore, *Messy Church*, London: Bible Reading Fellowship, 2006.

Baptism resources

Ally Barrett, *Making the Most of Your Child's Baptism: A gift for all the family*, London: SPCK, 2011.
Anne E. Kitch, *Taking the Plunge, Baptism and Parenting*, New York: Morehouse Publishing, 2006.

General

Robert Alter, *The Art of Biblical Narrative*, New York: Basic Books, 1981.
Robert Atwell, *Gift: 100 Readings for new parents*, Norwich: Canterbury Press, 2005.
Paul Bayes, Tim Sledge et al., *Mission-Shaped Parish*, London: Church House Publishing, 2006.
Common Worship: Services and Prayers for the Church of England, London: Church House Publishing, 2000.
Trevor Dennis, *Speaking of God*, London: SPCK, 1992.
John Drane, *The McDonaldization of the Church*, London: Darton, Longman and Todd, 2000.
Stephen Kuhrt, *Church Growth Through the Full Welcome of Children*, Cambridge: Grove Books, 2009.

Useful websites

www.startingrite.org

www.johnsonsbaby.co.uk
www.iaim.org.uk
www.ebay.co.uk
www.bookdepository.co.uk
www.amazon.co.uk
www.surestart.gov.uk
www.nhs.uk
www.gov.uk/free-early-education
www.theuglyducklingcompany.com